BELVOIR CASTLE

Emma Rutland

BELVOIR CASTLE

THE DUCHESS OF RUTLAND

with Jane Pruden

FRANCES LINCOLN LIMITED
PUBLISHERS

Frances Lincoln Limited
4 Torriano Mews
Torriano Avenue
London NW5 2RZ
www.franceslincoln.com

Belvoir Castle
Copyright © Frances Lincoln Limited 2009
Text copyright © Emma, The Duchess of Rutland 2009
Photographs © Emma, The Duchess of Rutland 2009
First Frances Lincoln edition 2009

A catalogue record for this book is available from the British Library.

ISBN 978-0-7112-3052-1

Designed by Anne Wilson

Printed and bound in China

9 8 7 6 5 4 3 2

PAGE 1 The silver-gilt Staunton Key, or Key of the Staunton
Tower, was presented to the Prince Regent on his visit to Belvoir
in 1813 by the Revd Dr Staunton; he presented it again to Queen
Victoria on her visit in 1843. It represents the key to the keep, or
stronghold, of the first castle, for which the Staunton family
provided the traditional guard.

PREVIOUS PAGES When it is seen silhouetted against the dawn
light, the castle looks so fantastical that it is almost like a
Hollywood version of a castle.

ABOVE Peacocks have been an emblem of the family and an
element of the crest since the 15th century. Here they are
depicted in the frieze in the Elizabeth Saloon.

RIGHT A vignette from the Elizabeth Saloon includes damask-silk
wall panels, Louis XIV French *boiserie* and a Regency side cabinet
inlaid with *pietra dura* details.

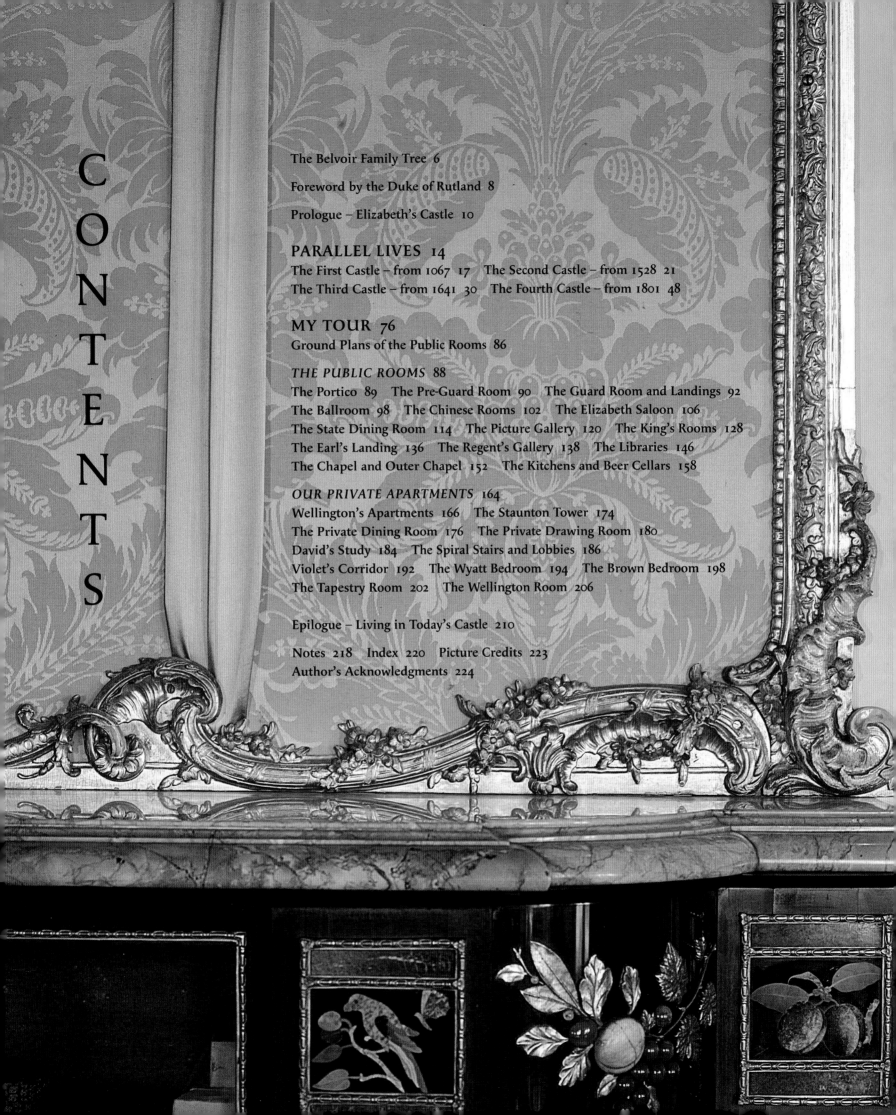

CONTENTS

The Belvoir Family

LEFT The coat of arms of Francis, 6th Earl of Rutland.
RIGHT The coat of arms of the Duke of Rutland.
The family motto is 'Pour Y Parvenir', which means
'To Obtain Your Object'.

Robert de Todeni *d.* 1088 = Adelais

Adeliza = Roger Bigot

Cecilia de Belvoir = William de Albini Brito (William de Albini I) *d. c.*1155

William de Albini II *d.* 1168 = Matilda de Senlis (*also known as* Maud de St Liz)

William de Albini III *d.* 1236 = (1) Margery, *daughter of Odinel de Umfranville*
(2) Agatha Trusbut

William de Albini IV *d.* 1247 = Albreda Biset

Robert de Ros, 1st Baron of Hamlake *d.* 1285 = Isabelle Albini *d.* 1301

William de Ros *d.* 1317 = Matilda, *daughter of John de Vaux*

William de Ros II *d.* 1342 = Margery de Badlesmere

William de Ros III *d.* 1352 = Margaret, *daughter of Ralph, Lord Neville*   Thomas de Ros *d.* 1383 = Beatrice, *daughter of Earl of Stafford*

John de Ros *d.* 1394 = Mary Percy *d.* 1395   Sir William de Ros *d.* 1414 = Margaret, *daughter of Earl of Arundel, d.* 1439

John, Lord Ros *d.* 1421 = Margaret, *daughter of Philip Despenser*   Thomas, Lord Ros *d.* 1431 = Eleanor, *daughter of Earl of Warwick*

Thomas, Lord Ros *d.* 1464 = Philippa, *daughter of John de Tiptoft*

Edmund, Lord Ros *d.* 1508   Eleanor *d.* 1487 = Sir Robert Manners *d. c.*1485   Isabel = Sir Thomas Lovell

Sir George Manners *d.* 1513 = Anne, *daughter of Sir Thomas Leger, d.* 1526

(1) Elizabeth, *daughter of Sir Robert Lovell* = Sir Thomas Manners, 1st Earl of Rutland *d.* 1543 = (2) Eleanor, *daughter of Sir William Paston, d.* 1551

Henry, 2nd Earl *d.* 1563 = (1) Margaret, *daughter of Earl of Westmorland, d.* 1560
(2) Bridget, *daughter of John, Lord Hussey of Sleaford, d.* 1600

Edward, 3rd Earl *d.* 1587 = Isabel, *daughter of Sir Thomas Holcroft*   John, 4th Earl *d.* 1588 = Elizabeth, *daughter of Sir Francis Charlton*

Roger, 5th Earl *d.* 1612 = Elizabeth, *daughter of Sir Philip Sidney, d.* 1612   Francis, 6th Earl *d.* 1632 = (1) Frances, *daughter of Sir Henry Knyvett*
= (2) Cecilia, *daughter of Sir John Tufton, d.* 1653

George, 7th Earl *d.* 1641 = Frances, *daughter of Sir Edward Carey, d.* 1641

Dorothy, *daughter of Sir George Vernon, d.* 1584 = Sir John Manners *d.* 1611

Sir George Manners of Haddon *d.* 1623 = Grace, *daughter of Sir Henry Pierrepont, d.* 1650

John, 8th Earl *d.* 1679 = Frances, *daughter of Lord Montagu, d.* 1671

(1) Anne Pierrepont, *daughter of Henry, Marquess of Dorchester* = John, 9th Earl, 1st Duke of Rutland *d.* 1711 = (3) Catherine Noel, *daughter of Viscount Campden, d.* 1732
(2) Diana Bruce, *daughter of Robert, Earl of Ailesbury, d.* 1672 =

(1) Katherine, *daughter of Lord William Russell, d.* 1711 = John, 2nd Duke *d.* 1721 = (2) Lucy, *daughter of Lord Sherrard*

John, 3rd Duke *d.* 1779 = Bridget Sutton, *daughter of Lord Lexington, d.* 1734

Frances Seymour, *daughter of Duke of Somerset, d.* 1760 = John, Marquis of Granby *d.* 1770

Charles, 4th Duke *d.* 1787 = Mary Isabella Somerset, *daughter of Duke of Beaufort, d.* 1831

Elizabeth Howard, *daughter of Frederick, Earl of Carlisle, d.* 1825 = John Henry, 5th Duke 1778–1857

Charles, 6th Duke 1815–88

(1) Catherine, *daughter of Col. George Marlay, d.* 1854 = John, 7th Duke 1818–1906 = (2) Janetta, *daughter of Thomas Hughan, d.* 1899

Henry John, 8th Duke 1852–1925 = Violet, *daughter of Col. Hon. C. H. Lindsay, d.* 1937

John, 9th Duke 1886–1940 = Kathleen, *daughter of Francis John Tennant, d.* 1989   *Children in addition to John:* Lord Haddon, Marjorie, Diana, Violet

Children in addition to Charles: Ursula *b.* 1916, Isobel 1918–2008, John 1922–2001, Roger *b.* 1925

Charles John Robert, 10th Duke 1919–99 = (1) Anne, *daughter of Maj. William Cumming-Bell* = (2) Frances, *daughter of Charles Sweeny*

Charlotte *b.* 1947   David Charles Robert, 11th Duke *b.* 1959 = Rachel Emma, *daughter of John Watkins*

Children: Violet *b.* 1993, Alice *b.* 1995, Eliza *b.* 1997, Charles *b.* 1999, Hugo *b.* 2003

Foreword

OUR FAMILY has lived at Belvoir for nearly 950 years. The estate has been passed down through 36 successive generations, mostly via primogeniture but on occasion through the female line – hence the name change to Manners in our early history. The castle was given the French name Belvoir – meaning beautiful view and now pronounced 'beaver' – by its first owner, Robert de Todeni, a Norman baron. He fought at the Battle of Hastings in 1066 as William the Conqueror's Standard Bearer and the beautiful site on which Belvoir stands was his reward. The castle that he built here was the first of four which have superseded each other over the centuries.

That first castle, which was begun in 1067, was constructed primarily to defend its Norman owners from attack, and so took full advantage of its defensive position high up on the ridge. It served its purpose, but by 1464 the Wars of the Roses had taken their toll and it was more or less in ruins. Some 60 years later it rose again, but as a nobler structure with a central courtyard, parts of which can still be recognised today. But in 1649 that too was destroyed, by Parliamentarians after Royalists had seized it during the Civil War. Its third incarnation, begun in 1654, was deliberately designed as a large family home with no connotations of defence or war.

The castle that you see today was built for the 5th Duke and Duchess of Rutland between 1801 and 1832. The Duchess, who came from Castle Howard, in Yorkshire, was distinctly unimpressed with the ordinariness of the Charles II house that she found when she arrived. What she wanted – and got, despite many setbacks, including a devastating fire – was a fairytale palace.

Belvoir remains one of the country's finest Regency castles, and we are enormously privileged to be able to call it home. It has a heritage of which I am very proud, and I am delighted to be able to share much of its history and its treasures in this book that my wife Emma has compiled so admirably.

Rutland

Prologue

Elizabeth's Castle

'The Castle stands high on a hill overlooking the vale of Belvoir, then a contented vale of solid farms and farmers who followed foxhounds and thought of their acres in terms of "runs," "jumps" and "coverts." The Duchess who had built this Valhalla was a Howard from Castle Howard and as a bride had been grievously disappointed at the low wandering Charles II house built on the foundations of a Norman strong-hold. She had expected better, so her kind rich husband allowed her to raze it to the ground and to build on the old foundations a real castle, a neo-Norman, neo-Gothic, neo-everything.'

So WROTE Lady Diana Cooper (née Manners, second daughter of the 8th Duke and Duchess of Rutland), in her first book of memoirs.[1]

The bride that Lady Diana Cooper describes is 18-year-old Lady Elizabeth Howard; the kind rich husband is John, the 21-year-old 5th Duke of Rutland. Elizabeth first arrived at Belvoir in 1799, just before her marriage and, according to legend, was horrified by the house that she was expected to live in. It was a squat, mid-17th-century mansion with no pretensions to grandeur but, more than that, it was almost in ruins, the furniture was scant and in disrepair, and only the pictures on the walls appeared to be worth salvaging. Adding to her misery, the staff seemed often to be drunk or even absent. It would have been a very stark contrast to her palatial childhood home at Castle Howard. Belvoir had been neglected chiefly because her father-in-law, the 4th Duke, had rarely lived there – he spent more time at Cheveley Park (another Rutland house, near Newmarket in Suffolk) and, when he was Lord Lieutenant of Ireland, in Dublin; not only did he inherit debts, but he spent any available funds on art, gambling and lavish entertaining; when he died in 1787 he left little money to his widow, and his son John, who became the 5th Duke, was only nine years old. However, by the time John married 12 years later he had developed a deep respect for his old family home – expressed in letters to his family – and he encouraged his young wife's plans to refashion the castle to her own taste. Luckily they seem to have fallen deeply in love – they wrote almost daily in the most gushing terms when they were apart – and perhaps he also wanted to make her happy.

Elizabeth began to develop a vision of how Belvoir should look as soon as she was married. It is likely that she even drew the amateurish plans of a 'Gothick'-style castle dated as early as 1799 found in the archives. She wanted a comfortable, new, fairytale castle that would reflect the prevailing Regency fashion for medievalism and, at the same time, echo its former history. Growing up at Castle Howard during the final stages of its construction may have inspired her architectural ambition. She found that her father-in-law had commissioned plans for the castle from Lancelot 'Capability' Brown in 1780, but that nothing had

Elizabeth, 5th Duchess of Rutland, **by George Sanders. The artist has somehow managed to capture Elizabeth's artistic sensibility, her strength of character and her incurable romanticism.**

been done about them. The discovery of these plans in the Belvoir Archives in 2008, long thought to have perished in the fire of 1816 that destroyed so much else, reveal more than anything else about about her intentions. Brown's schemes include detailed drawings of the third castle and the changes he proposed, as well as drawings for new gardens and parkland (see page 46). His ideas for the house, however, obviously did not satisfy her insatiable imagination and in 1801 she engaged the leading Gothic romantic architect James Wyatt, who was also working for the Prince Regent at Windsor Castle, to work at Belvoir. It is clear from comparing Brown's drawings with Wyatt's that, far from wishing to raze her new husband's family home to the ground as had previously been believed, she actually wanted to convert and embellish the original

building. Her fanciful ideas and Wyatt's expertise resulted in a scheme to transform the old house, and by Good Friday of that year work had begun.

Her husband instructed his close friend and private chaplain, the Revd John Thoroton, Rector of nearby Bottesford and a gifted amateur architect, to supervise the project. With their help, and with the passion and enthusiasm of youth and a deftness beyond her years and education, she embarked on building what is one of today's finest Regency manor houses in England. As John Martin Robinson, an architectural historian with a special knowledge of the period, said: 'Nowhere in the country is there a house that reflects all the fashionable styles of the period – Norman, Gothic, Roman, Renaissance, French and Chinese – so impressively and accurately as Belvoir.'

To me, the castle is Elizabeth's. She determined every room, every corridor, the view from every window; her personality feels deeply embedded in the fabric of this house. But what was she really like? Her beauty and diminutive frame belied a wilful and determined streak but her strongest asset was her femininity. Portraits reveal a fine woman with an air about her that must have been utterly compelling. Men were certainly attracted to her. Even in the earliest stages of her marriage she drew attention from admirers. Her husband's hunting friend, the notorious society dandy Beau Brummell, was particularly smitten.[2] As her marriage progressed, admirers – including the Duke of York – probably became lovers, but she never wavered in her loyalties and her first priority was always her family and home.

A frequent visitor to Belvoir was Mrs Arbuthnot, the mistress of the Duke of Wellington. Of Elizabeth she wrote, 'She certainly was a woman of extraordinary genius and talent mixed up with a great deal of vanity and folly', and added that she was, 'hated by all the fine ladies of London because she was far above them', and, although she had 'very few female friends, to those few she was most constant and affectionate'. Mrs Arbuthnot also gave us an insight into what Elizabeth looked like when she commented that the marble sculpture of Elizabeth that is now in the Elizabeth Saloon was 'excessively like her'.[3]

Elizabeth must have been determined and resourceful at an early age, since the Duke left her to cope on her own at Belvoir for months at a time. From October to April his interests, along with his regimental and public commitments, were non-negotiable: shooting and hunting. He spent the very first Christmas after they were married in London,[4] leaving her at Belvoir, the dilapidated house that she detested, to host a house party and cope with her first pregnancy; and he spent most of the winter riding to hounds from his hunting lodge in Lincolnshire.[5] She also had to keep up with the heavy demands of his social life: shooting and hunting parties at Belvoir were major fixtures in the calendar, and his birthdays were celebrated in the most spectacular manner. (His two-week-long coming-of-age party at Belvoir, just before his marriage, included a dinner for 4,000 people.)[6]

Her energy was prodigious. By 1816 she had produced eight babies (though she had to suffer the agony of burying three of them) and, as well as keeping abreast of all the building works, she ran the farm and estate, landscaped the garden and park along the lines that Brown had suggested, and also renovated Cheveley Park. After her death, Mrs Arbuthnot wrote: 'she will be a most dismal loss to her husband. She managed all his affairs for him; he did nothing himself, and his estates, his houses, his family, every thing was under her rule.'[7] By 1825 she had, with John Thoroton's help, rebuilt and repaired all the damage that the great fire had caused at Belvoir in 1816; formed a close, probably scandalous, relationship with the Duke of York, the Prince Regent's brother; and become involved in any number of large-scale building projects in London, including a Royal palace, a new quay on the north bank of the River Thames, a new entrance to Hyde Park Corner and other embellishments in the Royal Parks. Over the years she grew in self-esteem and was revered by those around her. Her husband's private chaplain, the Revd Irvin Eller, aptly described her 'as the pride and ornament of his renovated Castle'.

I imagine that Elizabeth would still feel very much at home at Belvoir today. It is remarkably well preserved. So many houses were altered in the Victorian era but at Belvoir the costs of the original building, and those for rebuilding after the fire, drained the family's finances. There was no spare cash to indulge in any expensive whims of fancy for many generations. The 8th Duchess, Violet, made comparatively few, and mostly cosmetic, changes and she was always sympathetic to Elizabeth's style. Very few rooms are still laid out exactly as Elizabeth would have known them but much of the bespoke furniture is complete and the whole effect is a powerful evocation of the Regency period, as well as of Elizabeth's remarkable persona.

View of Belvoir Castle, 1816, by J. M. W. Turner. Turner's vision is every inch the fairytale castle that had been so longed for by Elizabeth. Only months after this painting was finished, the castle was partially destroyed by a devastating fire.

PARALLEL LIVES

The First Castle

from 1067

THE FIRST PROPRIETORS OF BELVOIR 1067–1464

ROBERT DE TODENI, from Tosny on the Seine in Normandy, was the first of a long line of successive generations to live in a castle at Belvoir. He was one of William the Conqueror's greatest barons and, in recognition of his role as Standard Bearer at the Battle of Hastings in 1066, was granted lands and estates in 11 counties across England. The Normans deliberately awarded lands that were spread out so that neighbouring barons could join forces to defend the Crown when necessary, and yet rebellious individuals were deterred from forming significant armies of their own.

The original estate at Belvoir was created from the adoption of 35 manors in Lincolnshire and 16 in Leicestershire; part of it was formerly owned by a thane called Leofric. The mention of his name in the Domesday Book highlights how completely the ownership of lands in the region changed after the Norman Conquest. The Anglo-Saxon communities were torn apart forever and, not surprisingly, the new Norman settlers were challenged at every opportunity.

Lincolnshire was the second most populated county after Norfolk in 1086 and militant groups would have attacked regularly. Robert wisely built his Norman castle on the steep and prominently positioned limestone ridge overlooking Leicestershire, Nottinghamshire and Lincolnshire. The commanding views meant that all the arterial roads – the Fosseway, Sewstern Lane and the Great North Road – could easily be observed. The ancient labyrinth of tracks that twisted and turned to the castle's entrance also contributed to the effectiveness of the site. The only known documentation of its construction is an ancient seal made for Robert's great-great-grandson William de Albini IV, probably to commemorate the new crenellated curtain wall he had built in 1267. It shows a fairly crude picture of a quadrangular three-tiered keep with battlements surrounded by a massive wall. The original castle would have been a motte-and-bailey design: motte comes from the French word meaning raised earth mound, and bailey describes an enclosed courtyard. Early medieval castles were built in wood and over the years were replaced with stone.

ABOVE The only known picture of the first castle survives on this ancient seal made for William de Albini IV c.1267.
OPPOSITE Belvoir Castle today stands on the same prominent spot as its predecessors did, where for the first 580 years of its existence its key objective was to defend the neighbouring landscape.
PREVIOUS PAGES *View of Belvoir Castle from the South West with Belvoir Hunt in Full Cry*, 1730, by Thomas Badeslade. This spectacular illustration of the third castle also shows the layout of its 16th-century formal gardens and the statues, by Caius Cibber, positioned along the driveway.

Robert's embattled wall around his keep incorporated the castle's stronghold, the Staunton Tower, or turret as it would have been then. Since medieval times the chief of the stronghold, who provided the castle guard, had been a member of the Staunton family. He would have been called on to raise men to defend the castle in times of crisis. He and his successors were, by law, wards to the Lord of Belvoir until Charles II put an end to feudal rights. The Staunton family still lives at Staunton Hall, 10 miles from here, and the head of the family is still entitled to bring the 'key of the Staunton Tower' to any visiting member of the Royal family, in honour of the ancient tenure.

Having built his castle and established himself at Belvoir, Robert appeared to have considered his spirituality and followed the medieval custom of endowing religious orders with surplus profits from land holdings. In 1077, having consulted his friend the noted Archbishop of Canterbury, Lanfranc, he built Belvoir Priory at the foot of the hill (close to the present Dower House), for four Black Monks of the order of St Benedict as a daughter cell to the Abbey of St Albans. The monks would have provided religious instruction, prayers for the souls of many local benefactors and medical attention for their neighbours. Robert de Todeni died in 1088 and was buried at the Priory. The remains of his body lay undisturbed until labourers excavated the site in 1726. His coffin, still visibly inscribed 'Robert de Todeni, le Fundeur', was later laid to rest in our Chapel.

Belvoir Castle passed through the female line via Robert de Todeni's daughter Adeliza, and her daughter Cecilia, to Cecilia's husband, William de Albini (or d'Aubigny) Brito.

William's grandson, also William de Albini, was one of the 25 barons who most prominently opposed King John's rule when, in 1215, they put their names to one of the most significant constitutional documents in political history: the Magna Carta. Having signed a charter that ostensibly left

him with greatly reduced power, the King quickly renounced the contract and within months was seeking revenge on the rebels. The barons appointed William de Albini as Governor of Rochester Castle, in Kent. This became the scene of a siege of the barons' troops by the King and his armies. Unfortunately for William, the barons were defeated after almost two long, expensive months. King John intended to have them all hanged but to avoid further unrest he settled for incarcerating them in Corfe Castle, on the Isle of Purbeck in Dorset. He made a conditional pact in 1216 with William's son Nicholas: in exchange for not executing his father, Belvoir would be confiscated and 6,000 marks would be required to secure William's release. This sum was raised by William's wife, who had to sell a considerable portion of their lands to do so.

The Albini name survived until 1247 when William de Albini IV died. His only surviving child, Isabelle, married a Yorkshire man, Robert de Ros, 1st Baron of Hamlake (or Helmsley today), probably in 1257. Their union was mutually advantageous: she was an heiress in her own right, and the de Ros family brought two considerable fortunes to the match. These included the patronage of Kirkham Priory and of Rievaulx Abbey, both in Yorkshire, which would reap enormous financial rewards in the 1530s following Henry VIII's dissolution of the monasteries.

This marriage introduced a Scottish connection: Robert de Ros was related to Alexander III, King of Scotland, who employed him in Scotland in 1258 to protect the Crown from rebellion in 1258. Fortunately Lord Ros was successful. In 1264 he joined the barons who, under Simon de Montfort, defeated Henry III's English forces at Lewes, in Sussex; but when the barons were themselves later defeated, he was imprisoned in Hungerford Castle, in Wiltshire. By 1267 the rebels and Henry had agreed peace terms and Lord Ros was released but Belvoir was again

ABOVE The Todeni coat of arms in the Guard Room.

subjected to the threat of confiscation, prompting Ros to improve the battlements in that year.

His son William de Ros succeeded to Belvoir on the death of his mother Isabelle in 1301. As the great-grandson of Isabel, daughter of William I, 'The Lion', King of Scotland, he had competed, though unsuccessfully, for the crown of Scotland in 1292. He later acquired large estates in Norfolk and Lincolnshire through his marriage to Matilda, daughter of John de Vaux, thus contributing considerably to the wealth of the Belvoir estate. He died in 1317 and was buried at Kirkham Priory.

His son, also named William de Ros, was appointed Lord High Admiral and was among those commissioned by the Archbishop of York to keep the peace between Edward II and Robert the Bruce, King of Scotland.

His son, another William de Ros, had a short but brave life. He is remembered for the heroic part he played in the Hundred Years War (1337–1453) which dragged on through the reigns of five English and French monarchs all fighting for control of France. He fought at Arguillon in 1346 when he was 19 years old and was knighted for his efforts. He fought again at Crécy in 1346 and at Calais in 1347. He died in 1352, on his way to the Holy Land to fight the Saracens with Henry Duke of Lancaster; he was only 26.

The castle had enjoyed a relatively peaceful existence for almost a hundred years from the mid-1300s and survived the damaging effects of the Black Death in the Vale of Belvoir when much land became neglected as a result of the high mortality rate. Successive generations of the family continued to prosper at Belvoir. Thomas de Ros of Hamlake, William's brother and heir, accompanied the King of Cyprus to the Holy Land in 1364 and fought in France between 1369 and 1371. His eldest son and heir, John, Lord Ros of Hamlake, was knighted in 1377 at the coronation of Richard II, the ten-year-old son of the Black Prince, and died in Cyprus in 1394 on his way to a pilgrimage in Jerusalem. Another son, Sir William de Ros, succeeded his brother at the age of 24 and was among those who negotiated a peace treaty with Scotland. Sir William de Ros' son John, Lord Ros, succeeded him in 1414 but was killed with his brother William at the Battle of Baugé in France, in 1421. A third brother, Thomas, Lord Ros, succeeded and later received a knighthood for his valour in the wars in France.

Two years after the end of the exhausting and costly war with France, civil war erupted at home. Known to us as the Wars of the Roses (1455–85), it was a struggle for the throne between the supporters of the House of York (whose emblem was a white rose) and those who supported the House of Lancaster (whose emblem was a red rose). The next Thomas, Lord Ros, was a Lancastrian and in 1461, following a victory of the Yorkists led by Edward IV, he was executed and the castle and lordship of Belvoir, together with a large portion of his estates and grants, were bequeathed to William, Lord Hastings, a key Yorkist. When Hastings arrived to claim his castle Ros's supporters, led by Mr Harington from nearby Exton, attacked and drove him away. He withdrew, but returned a second time with enough forces to pillage the castle: he stripped the lead from the roofs and removed the stone for use on his own property in Ashby de la Zouch, in west Leicestershire. The castle was left in ruins.

Nearly twenty years after the defeat of the Yorkists and following the accession of Henry VII in 1485, the Belvoir properties and the ruined castle were restored to the Ros family after the late Thomas's son Edmund, Lord Ros, had successfully petitioned Parliament. Although the family were finally reunited with their estates, the achievement was not without caveat: the estates were divided up, with portions given to other members of the family, in particular to Edmund's younger sister Isabel, wife of Sir Thomas Lovell who was a powerful influence at Court.

ABOVE The arms representing the marriage between William de Albini II and Matilda de Senlis in the Guard Room.

ABOVE LEFT The tomb of William de Ros, 1414, in Bottesford Church. The peacock is already an integral element in the design of the family tomb.

ABOVE RIGHT The tomb of John, Lord Ros, 1421, in Bottesford Church.

BELOW The Ros coat of arms dating from the 15th century in Bottesford Church.

Nine years later Isabel audaciously presented a petition to Parliament, stating that Edmund was not fit to fulfil his responsibilities and requesting that her husband might have the guidance and governance over her brother. Poor Edmund, having returned from abroad to reclaim his birthright after the disputes between the Lancastrians and Yorkists had been resolved, found himself outcast and living at Elsings, a property in Enfield, Middlesex, inherited from his mother. He died without an heir in 1508 and was buried in the churchyard of that parish.

His inheritance had passed to his eldest sister, Eleanor, who married Sir Robert Manners of Ethall, Northumberland. By marrying Eleanor, Sir Robert acquired Belvoir, Hamlake (Helmsley) in Yorkshire and Orston in Nottinghamshire. His eldest son became Sir George Manners, Lord Ros. He achieved fame during a battle to defend England from the Scots, earning a knighthood from the Earl of Surrey, who was General of the Army, and finding favour with Henry VII. His loyalty to the Tudors continued, and Henry VIII was with him when George fell sick and died after the siege at Tournay in France in 1513. But it was his marriage to Anne St Leger, daughter of Anne Plantagenet, that had the greatest significance for his descendants. Anne was the niece of Edward IV and of his brothers Richard III and Edmund, Earl of Rutland; this connection undoubtedly helped elevate the Manners' family financially, politically and socially in Royal circles. Certainly George's close relationship with Henry VII would have benefited the family, as did that of George's son Thomas with Henry VIII. George and Anne were buried in St George's Chapel at Windsor Castle.

The Second Castle

from 1528

THE 1ST EARL OF RUTLAND, THOMAS MANNERS, 1513–43

THE SECOND CASTLE was built on the strength of the family's spectacular good fortune. George's son, Sir Thomas Manners, Lord Ros, was created Earl of Rutland in 1525. The earldom had formerly been a Royal title and bestowing it upon Thomas was an acknowledgment of his close relationship to Edward IV and Richard III, his maternal great-uncles. At the same time the lions and fleur de lys were added to his coat of arms by permission of Henry VIII.

Sir Thomas acquired great wealth during the second quarter of the 16th century, firstly on the death of his great-uncle, Sir Thomas Lovell. Lovell's lands and estates obtained from his brother-in-law Edmund, Lord Ros, were left to Thomas and his first wife, Eleanor Lovell, who was a niece of Sir Thomas. Further wealth was acquired after 1536 following the dissolution of the monasteries and sale of abbeys and priories to raise money for the Crown. The Albini and the Ros families had

BELOW LEFT The Earl of Rutland's shield in Bottesford Church. The lions and fleur de lys were added in recognition of the 1st Earl's connection with Anne Plantagenet, who was his maternal grandmother.

BELOW RIGHT An outline of the second castle was presented as a tapestry by Lady Victoria Manners in the early part of the 20th century. She copied this from a tapestry map sewn in 1632 by a Miss Mary Eyre during a stay at Grove Hall, in Nottinghamshire.

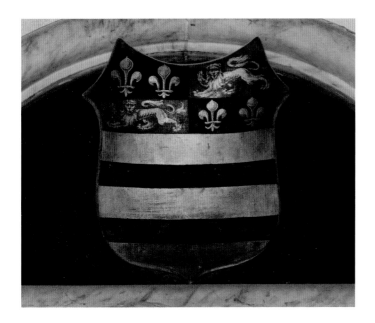

RIGHT The tomb of the 3rd Earl and his wife Isabel in Bottesford Church.
FAR RIGHT A detail from the 2nd Earl's tomb in Bottesford Church.
BELOW *Sir Thomas Manners, 1st Earl of Rutland*, mid-1670s, by Jeremiah van der Eyden. The 9th Earl of Rutland commissioned van der Eyden to paint a set of portraits of all the earls. These now hang together on the Earl's Landing.
OPPOSITE *Henry Manners, 2nd Earl of Rutland*, mid-1670s, by Jeremiah van der Eyden. Henry was a courtier who served Edward IV, Queen Mary and Elizabeth I.

founded many priories and abbeys in the 11th and 12th centuries, and the 1st Earl of Rutland was able to acquire large tracts of their former estates, including Belvoir and Kirkham Priories and Rievaulx Abbey, in exchange for other lands.

With his new-found wealth, the 1st Earl decided to rebuild the Norman castle at Belvoir, which had been in ruins since 1464, but as a nobler structure with a quadrangular building surrounding a central courtyard. Work probably started around 1528 when the King's master mason, John Redman, who had previously worked on Hampton Court Palace for Cardinal Wolsey, was asked to quote for the construction. It was completed in 1543. Little is known about it and there is even less illustrated documentation. We do know, however, that much of the stone to build it came from Croxton Abbey, in Leicestershire, and Belvoir Priory after they were demolished following the dissolution of the monasteries.

Thomas, 1st Earl of Rutland, was more a diplomat than a real mover and shaker and his relatively minor role in politics probably secured his head and the lineage. He was a loyal subject to Henry VIII, regularly playing tennis and competing in jousting tournaments with him when they were younger and being a faithful courtier for the rest of his life. So great was Henry VIII's trust in him that he was made Lord Chamberlain to three of Henry's wives: Jane Seymour, Anne of Cleves and Catherine Howard. Thomas's second wife, Eleanor Paston (from Norfolk), was honoured by being allowed to travel in a coach following Jane Seymour's funeral procession. Despite Thomas's own Catholic faith, he remained supportive of the King during both Henry's divorces, first from Catherine of Aragon, and later from Anne of Cleves. A letter from Thomas to the Lord Privy Seal notes that Rutland had been summoned to speak to Anne soon after 4 o'clock in the morning, with reference to the King's intention to divorce her. Seeing her 'take the matter heavily', he had 'desired her to be of good comfort', assuring her that Henry was 'so good and virtuous a prince' that he [the King] desired nothing which was not comfortable to the law of God and the dictates of his conscience and necessary for the future quietness of the realm.'[8] Thomas died in 1543, just four years before the King, and was buried near his newly built castle, in neighbouring Bottesford Church.

THE 2ND EARL OF RUTLAND, HENRY MANNERS, 1543–63

HENRY, the eldest son from Thomas's second marriage (his first marriage was childless), became the 2nd Earl of Rutland. Thomas left a hundred estates and manors, and the income from the Yorkshire estates alone amounted to £2,400 per annum. However, in his will he stipulated that his wealth should be divided and a share should go to his wife and their other children. In addition, his debts and building costs had escalated, and Henry had to sell the family's land in Northumberland, and the Ethall estate was passed to the Crown to repay debts.

To keep the family's variable fortunes in perspective, however, it is interesting to note that in Lawrence Stone's book *Family and Fortune,* based on extensive research in the Belvoir archives in 1970s, the Rutlands were still reported to be one of the five wealthiest families in England in the 1550s after the dissolution of the monasteries.

Henry was well respected by the Protestant Edward VI and bore the King's spurs at his coronation, an esteemed privilege. But Edward's life was short and the position of the church, fluctuating between Catholic and Protestant control, during this Tudor period demanded the utmost discretion from courtiers. Henry's wife, Margaret Neville, was a staunch Catholic, which suited his position at court during Queen Mary's reign. Like his father and grandfather, he was diplomatic and he managed to avoid any life-threatening confrontation. Despite temporarily siding with Lady Jane Grey's claim to the throne, he was quick to declare support to the passionately Catholic Queen Mary when she came to power. His vacillations cost him a heavy fine of 1,000 marks and a three-month custodial sentence but, after his release, he was soon back in favour with the Queen. The fact that his mother, Eleanor Paston, was a favoured member of Mary's court must have had some influence.

By the time Elizabeth I was crowned, Henry was back in his comfort zone with the church under Protestant control. His prominent position at the coronation and his creation as Knight of the Garter in 1559 cemented his relationship with the Crown. His second marriage to the fervently Protestant Bridget Hussey in 1563, following the death of his first wife Margaret, would have helped him too. He was appointed President of her Majesty's Council of the North by Elizabeth, and his wisdom and loyalty were tested in the borders as forces were recruited to patrol the northern frontier from French armies sent to support Mary Queen of Scots' continual threat to the English throne.

He died suddenly in 1563, leaving debts of £5,600 caused by his extremely high standard of living, building costs and huge expenses incurred from his employ in the north. The sale of part of the estate was averted by a grant of £1,800 that his executors, through their connections at Court, managed to obtain from the Crown. His 14-year-old son Edward, 3rd Earl of Rutland, was left in the capable guardianship of William Cecil, later Lord Burghley.

THE 3RD AND 4TH EARLS OF RUTLAND, EDWARD MANNERS, 1563–87, AND JOHN MANNERS, 1587–88

HAVING BENEFITED from Cecil's guardianship, an education and travels to France, Edward failed to take up a future in law as Cecil had hoped, and instead settled into local politics. However, he must have retained influence in Court circles because he was one of a group charged with negotiating a treaty between Scotland and England and resolving the problem of the Catholic Mary Queen of Scots' claim to the English throne. Edward was sent to Berwick, on the borders, to broker the deal. The resulting Treaty of

Berwick, signed in 1586, successfully pledged an alliance between the two countries, uniting them against any threat from foreign powers, particularly Spain and France. At the same time the Protestant James VI of Scotland (later James I of England) accepted an annuity of £4,000 – a considerable addition to his paltry income – whereby he tacitly acknowledged his position as Elizabeth's heir. The Queen was so impressed with Edward that she proposed making him the next Lord Chancellor but he died the following year. He was 38.

During his lifetime Edward had managed to add to the family's wealth once again, despite buying many new books for the library at Belvoir, spending extensively on two of his other estates, Newark Castle and Helmsley in Yorkshire, and acquiring two new manors. He had married Isabel Holcroft, daughter of Sir Thomas Holcroft from Chester, and they had one child, Elizabeth, also a ward of Lord Burghley. She inherited the Ros title (which had been able to pass through the female line since the 13th century) and became Baroness Ros, while Edward's brother John succeeded as the 4th Earl of Rutland in 1587.

John died only a year after his brother – and the day after he had written his will. He had been appointed constable of Nottingham Castle and Lord Lieutenant of Nottinghamshire on his succession. Three of his sons succeeded to the earldom; the first, Roger, aged only 11 became the 5th Earl of Rutland.

THE 5TH EARL OF RUTLAND, ROGER MANNERS, 1588–1612

ROGER WAS EDUCATED at Queens' and Corpus Christi Colleges, Cambridge, receiving an MA in 1595. A two-year tour of Europe, travelling through the Low Countries, Germany, Switzerland and France, followed. He then studied at Padua University, in Italy, and at Gray's Inn, in 1598. During his time at Cambridge he met Robert

FAR LEFT *Edward Manners, 3rd Earl of Rutland*, mid-1670s, by Jeremiah van der Eyden.
LEFT *John Manners, 4th Earl of Rutland*, mid-1670s, by Jeremiah van der Eyden.

Devereux, the 2nd Earl of Essex, and Henry Wriothesley, the Earl of Southampton, who was Shakespeare's first patron. A number of writers and historians have suggested that Roger Manners may have contributed to or even written some of Shakespeare's work. Claims to the authorship have a history that goes back to Francis Bacon – other candidates include the Earl of Oxford, Christopher Marlowe and Ben Jonson. But the general view is that the 5th Earl was 'too young and unproven' to have used Shakespeare's persona as a cover for his own work. There are no contemporary accounts of Rutland's literary efforts or being involved in writing other than taking part in plays written anonymously by the students at Cambridge while an undergraduate, although his wife, Elizabeth Sidney (daughter of Philip Sidney, author of *Arcadia*), is said to have been a poet and they both mixed in literary circles and enjoyed taking part in Court masques. The absence of hard evidence suggests it is likely that the 5th Earl and Countess of Rutland were merely acquaintances of William Shakespeare and that through meetings and during the course of correspondence with mutual friends, ideas emerged that were later echoed in his work.

Early in Rutland's life the Earl of Essex (Elizabeth Sidney's stepfather) became his mentor. When Rutland went abroad on a precursor to a Grand Tour Essex wrote him at least three private letters of travel advice. These letters inspired another letter of travel advice from Essex to Rutland, but this time intended for public circulation as a form of political propaganda to demonstrate Essex's statesmanship.

In defence of Queen Elizabeth's orders, Rutland and his younger brother George Manners joined Essex's badly organized, ill-fated Irish expedition in 1599. Rutland served as Colonel of Foot and was knighted by Essex at Cahir Castle, in Tipperary, Ireland, on 30 May 1599. On his return to England, however, he was kept out of prison only by the intervention of his friends who had influence with Elizabeth. In February 1601 he and his younger brothers, Francis, later 6th Earl of Rutland, and Sir George Manners, played prominent parts in Essex's final rebellion against Elizabeth. When it failed, all three brothers were imprisoned in the Tower of London; a fine of 1,000 marks each (which was later retracted) was imposed on the younger two; Rutland was fined £30,000 and was exiled from Belvoir and confined to the house of his uncle,

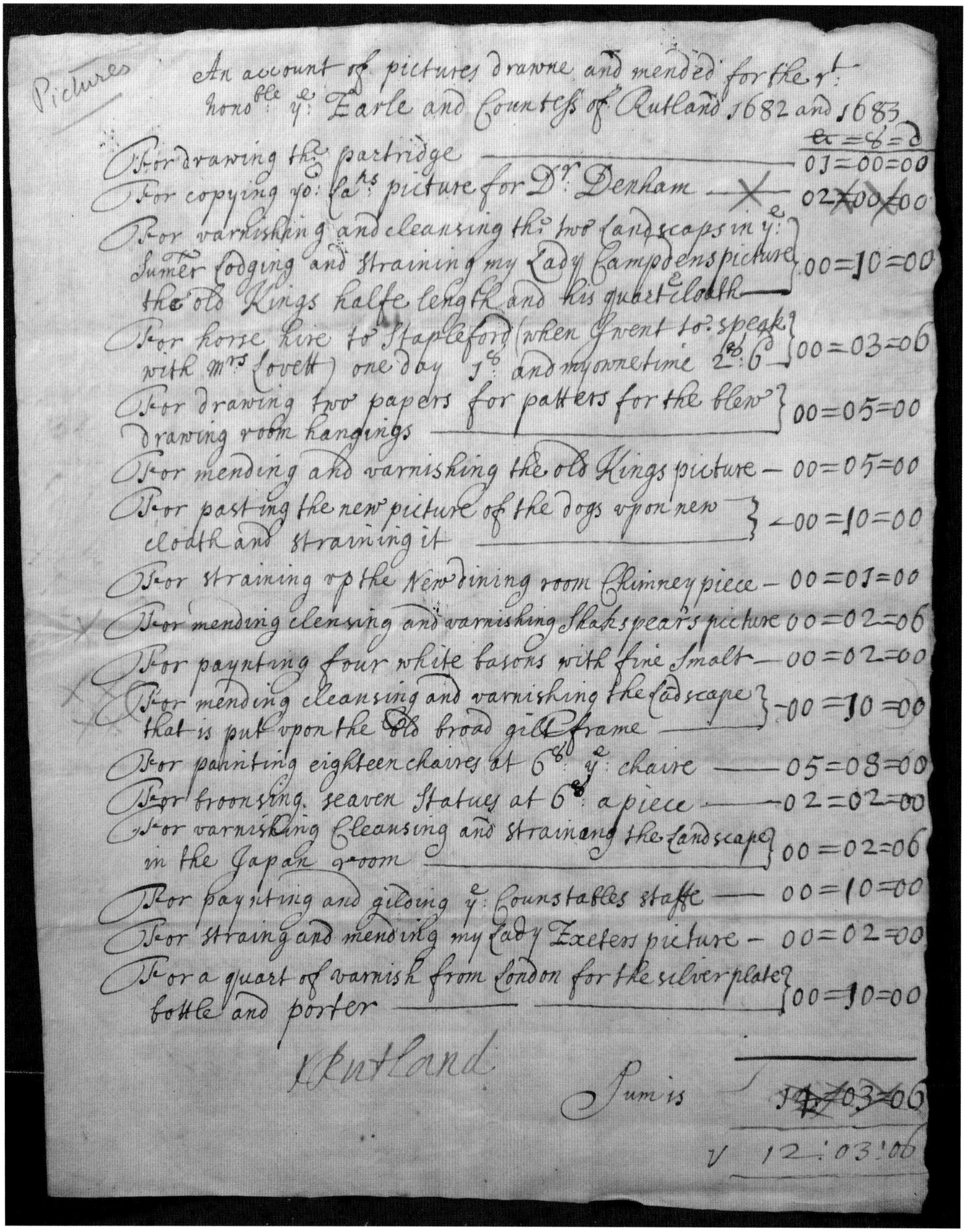

Pictures

An account of pictures drawne and mended for the rt.
honoble ye Earle and Countess of Rutland 1682 and 1683

	£ = s = d
For drawing the partridge	01 = 00 = 00
For copying yor Lats picture for Dr. Denham ✗	~~02 = 00 = 00~~
For varnishing and cleansing the two landscaps in ye Sumer lodging and straining my Lady Campdens picture the old Kings halfe length and his quart cloath	00 = 10 = 00
For horse hire to Stapleford (when I went to speak with Mrs Lovett) one day 1s and my owne time 2s:6d	00 = 03 = 06
For drawing two papers for patters for the blew drawing room hangings	00 = 05 = 00
For mending and varnishing the old Kings picture	00 = 05 = 00
For pasting the new picture of the dogs vpon new cloath and straining it	00 = 10 = 00
For straining vp the New dining room Chimney piece	00 = 01 = 00
For mending cleansing and varnishing Shakspears picture	00 = 02 = 06
For paynting four white basons with fine Smalt	00 = 02 = 00
For mending cleansing and varnishing the landscape that is put vpon the old broad gilt frame	00 = 10 = 00
For painting eighteen chaires at 6d ye chaire	05 = 08 = 00
For broonsing seaven Statues at 6d a piece	02 = 02 = 00
For varnishing cleansing and straining the landscape in the Japan groom	00 = 02 = 06
For paynting and gilding ye Counstables staffe	00 = 10 = 00
For straing and mending my Lady Exeters picture	00 = 02 = 00
For a quart of varnish from London for the silver plate bottle and porter	00 = 10 = 00

Rutland

Sum is ~~14~~ 03 = 06

V 12 : 03 : 06

Roger Manners, in Uffington, in Lincolnshire. Rutland's head was saved by direct intervention from this uncle, who had fortuitously had a long and illustrious career at Court. Essex's head was not saved; he was executed that year.

Thanks to the involvement of his uncle, the 3rd Earl, in the Treaty of Berwick, the 5th Earl was on good terms with James I, and was able to play host to the new King, at Belvoir on his journey from Edinburgh to London to take the English throne in 1603, entertaining him with feasting, dancing, singing, amateur theatricals and, of course, hunting across the Vale. During the King's stay, 40 members of the local gentry were knighted at Belvoir, and many more Royal visits to Belvoir ensued. As a mark of the King's favour, Rutland was chosen to go to Denmark to bestow the Order of the Garter upon Christian IV, the King's brother-in-law, and to attend the baptism of the latter's son on James's behalf. On his return he was made Lord Lieutenant of Lincolnshire and Steward of the Manor of Grantham, owned by James' wife, Queen Anne, further establishing his position as a magnate in the East Midlands.

He withdrew from Court life more and more in the last decade of his life, possibly because of ill-health, and died aged only 35 from stroke-like symptoms. His widow Elizabeth died two months later amid uncomfortable rumours of poisoning (a type of rumour common at that time). She had had many admirers including Sir Thomas Overbury, who did succumb to poisoning two years after Elizabeth's death whilst a prisoner in the Tower of London. His death refuelled speculation of perhaps a closer involvement with Roger's wife, but the Manners' childless marriage was widely understood to have been an unhappy one.

The near-fatal consequences of the expensive skirmishes of Roger's younger days, which could have ruined the entire Rutland family, had precipitated a less reckless approach to his life. By the time James I ascended the throne, Rutland's unpaid fine had been written off and, thanks to 'the great size of the (Rutland) annual income'[9] and fines for re-leasing the bulk of the estate when he came of age, he managed to clear his debts with only minor land sales, thus retrieving the Rutland financial position by the time of his death. His brother Francis inherited full coffers when he succeeded to the title and became the 6th Earl of Rutland in 1612.

LEFT William Shakespeare was said to have been an acquaintance of the 5th Earl and may even have stayed at Belvoir but there is no proof. There was a portrait of him at the castle but it was burnt in the fire of 1816. An invoice for cleaning the picture, between 1682 and 1683, for the 9th Earl and Countess of Rutland, was found by the 9th Duke in an abandoned room in the Estate Office (and was annotated by him). It is all that we now have to show for it.

RIGHT *Roger Manners, 5th Earl of Rutland*, mid-1670s, by Jeremiah van der Eyden. Roger mixed in both Court and literary circles and was an associate of William Shakespeare. Foreign Office and Manners family records show that he was the English Ambassador to the Danish Court at the same time that Shakespeare was writing *Hamlet*.

THE 6TH AND 7TH EARLS OF RUTLAND, FRANCIS MANNERS, 1612–32, AND GEORGE MANNERS, 1632–41

IF THERE IS ONE STORY in our locality that excites curiosity more than any other it is the tale of the alleged curse on the 6th Earl of Rutland's family by the witches of Belvoir. The Earl married twice and produced three children. His two sons by his second wife Cecilia both died in their youth in suspicious circumstances, convincing him that they had been the victims of witchcraft by two former employees, Margaret and Phillipa Flower, and their mother, Joan. The inscription on his tomb reads: 'He married Lady Cecilia Hungerford: daughter to ye Honourable Knight Sir John Tufton by whom he had two sonnes, both which dyed in their infancy by wicked practise & sorcerye'.

The three members of the Flower family were arrested and sent to Lincoln prison in 1618. The girls confessed to casting spells on the Rutland family and were hanged as witches on 11 March 1619 a year before the death of their

BELOW LEFT *Francis Manners, 6th Earl of Rutland*, mid-1670s, by Jeremiah van der Eyden.
BELOW RIGHT *Frances Knyvett, Countess of Rutland*, attributed to Marcus Gheeraedts. She was the 6th Earl of Rutland's first wife and mother of his only surviving child, Katherine.

second child, Francis. Their mother Joan, while awaiting trial, asked for bread and butter: 'If I am guilty of witchcraft, may this bread and butter never go through me.'[10] She ate the bread and dropped dead.

The Earl spent his life between Belvoir Castle and Court playing his part as local magnate, improving his estates and hunting, often with James I, who was a regular visitor. Like his brother Roger, he was educated at Cambridge University and travelled extensively before joining him on Lord Essex's failed coup against Elizabeth I. His only surviving child, Lady Katherine Manners, from his first marriage to Frances Knyvett – who herself had been co-heir to her father's fortune – was reputed to be the richest heiress in England (after Royalty) when she married George Villiers, later 1st Duke of Buckingham and favourite of James I, in 1620. He died in 1632 at Bishop's Stortford in Hertfordshire on his way from London to Belvoir and was succeeded by his brother Sir George Manners, as the 7th Earl of Rutland.

George, the 7th Earl, was 52 when he inherited the title. Most of the remaining nine years of his life were spent sorting out his brother's complicated will. He had married Frances Carey but they had no children. He died in 1641, having led what seems to have been an uneventful life, though the Revd Eller claims, in his book of 1841, that he hosted a Royal visit from Charles I in 1634.

ABOVE *Katherine Manners, Duchess of Buckingham, c.1633*, by Sir Anthony van Dyck. A miniature of her murdered husband, the Duke of Buckingham, is attached to her dress.
RIGHT *George Manners, 7th Earl of Rutland*, mid-1670s, by Jeremiah van der Eyden.

The Third Castle

from 1641

THE 8TH EARL OF RUTLAND, JOHN MANNERS, 1641–79

BECAUSE THERE WERE NO MALE HEIRS from the previous three earls, the title passed to a distant cousin. The 2nd Earl's brother, Sir John Manners, had married Dorothy Vernon, daughter of Sir George Vernon, the owner of Haddon Hall in the Derbyshire Peak district (and known locally as 'King of the Peak'), in 1563, and the grandson of this union, also named John Manners, became the 8th Earl of Rutland. For all his new status, he preferred to be known as Squire of Haddon and it seems that he was somewhat reticent about his elevation, despite its inevitability. He was 37 years old, already married to Frances Montagu[11] with at least 12 children, and had probably lived very comfortably at Haddon Hall. But, to Belvoir, the new Earl brought a much-needed source of income from his profitable Derbyshire estates. The honeymoon period for the castle, however, was short: almost as soon as the Earl had moved into Belvoir, civil war broke out, and events soon forced him to abandon it.

Considered to be only a moderate Parliamentarian, the Earl was nevertheless one of the 22 peers at Westminster who, in 1642–3, declined to attend Charles I in Oxford. In the ensuing conflict, Belvoir fell swiftly to the Royalists – through an act of stunning betrayal from a former employee, Sir Gervase Lucas. Lucas had been the Earl's Master of Horse but left his employ to support the King. While the Earl was away a hundred Royalist soldiers, under Lucas's command, took control of the lightly garrisoned castle on 28 January 1643. Belvoir then became a base for Royalist troops and operated as a refuge – King Charles even stayed a night there on his way into Lincolnshire – as well as a prison and a hospital.

The Earl, perhaps not the member of my husband's family of whom we are most proud, kept his head down and spent most of his time at Haddon and in London. He was so determined to avoid confrontation that he even feigned illness in order to be excused from difficult sessions in Westminster.

Five months after Charles was beheaded in January 1649 Belvoir Castle was destroyed by the orders of Cromwell's Parliament as they had no further use for it. The Council of

State reported that the Earl was content with this decision, having accepted £2,000 in compensation for the loss of both his castle and revenue from his lands occupied by troops.[12] In reality this did not amount to much; by the time rents to Parliament had been offset against it, very little was left. The 8th Earl, who was so fond of Haddon Hall, was happy to go back to live there but his wife had other ideas. She wanted to build a replacement for Belvoir and John Webb, a pupil of Inigo Jones, was commissioned to draw up plans for a palatial new residence.

The Earl was said to have had a preference for a house at Croxton instead of a new castle but his wife was clearly a determined character and work began on the third family seat at Belvoir in 1654. It wasn't all brand new. Some

remnants of the old castle still existed and the Countess's new home developed from the solid old foundations around the former courtyard. The embattled wall, the 15th-century medieval towers and some of the building in the west wing were all incorporated into the design. A second-storey

OPPOSITE An 18th-century view of Haddon Hall with the village of Bakewell in the background, by John Smith of Derby.
ABOVE LEFT *John Manners, the 8th Earl of Rutland,* mid-1670s, by Jeremiah van der Eyden.
ABOVE RIGHT *Frances Montagu, Countess of Rutland,* c.1706, English School. She was responsible for the third castle, insisting on building it on the site of the second castle, which had been destroyed during the Civil War.

ABOVE *View of Belvoir Castle*, 1744, by Jan Griffier the Younger. The Countess of Rutland instructed the architect John Webb to build the third castle without any reference to its predecessor's purpose. The result was a palatial two-storey Charles II house with new stables at the foot of the hill. The stables complex is still in use today.

bedroom floor was added; it was given a straight parapet in order to lose the impression of a castle and to look more like a house. The north front had steps up to a simple entrance and formal gardens were laid out with statues and plantations to complement the new scheme. The new stables that were built still exist. It was finished in 1668 and cost £11,730. Webb supervised the rebuilding and controlled the plans, which included detailed layouts of interior rooms. In 1661, a year after the restoration of the Crown to Charles II, the Earl was made Lord Lieutenant of Leicestershire. He died at Haddon in September 1679 and was buried at Bottesford, near his Countess.

LEFT A model of the Charles II castle was made in 1799 by the Revd William Mounsey, a curate at Bottesford Church. The north elevation (far left) had steps down the terraces, which were demolished in c.1801 as part of James Wyatt's design for the fourth castle. The south-west front (near left) was also mostly demolished in c.1801.

THE REVD IRVIN ELLER, chaplain to the 5th Duke and historian of Belvoir, writes of the 9th Earl of Rutland, later the 1st Duke of Rutland: 'The predilections of this noble Earl were entirely for the pleasures and pursuits of a rural life. And being possessed of a magnificent fortune, he could exercise to the fullest extent, the old English hospitality, which he greatly affected.'[13] It is true that the Earl lived an extravagant lifestyle and entertained his many guests lavishly at Belvoir, his primary residence. He loved hunting (he dressed his huntsmen in green), and his entourage was reported to be the largest of any nobleman in the country.

But his life was not just one big party. He married Lady Anne, eldest daughter and co-heir of Henry Pierrepont, Marquis of Dorchester, in 1658. Regrettably for

BELOW LEFT *John Manners as a boy with his Mother Frances, Countess of Rutland, c.1646, by Daniel Mytens. John became the 9th Earl and 1st Duke of Rutland.*
BELOW RIGHT *John Manners, 9th Earl of Rutland,* by Johann Clostermann, painted before he was created the 1st Duke of Rutland in 1703.

Lord Ros – as he was styled before becoming the 9th Earl – she turned out to be a serial adulteress. A formal separation from 'bed and board' was secured after only five years of marriage. A scandalous divorce, one of the first since Henry VIII's, was granted by private Acts of Parliament in 1667 and 1670 which prevented their children from inheriting any of his or his father's wealth, and allowed him to remarry. He married again in 1671 but, tragically, lost his second wife, Lady Diana Bruce of Staunton Harold, and a son, Robert, in childbirth in 1672. He then married Catherine Noel, daughter of Baptist Noel, Viscount Campden, in 1674 and had two sons and two daughters.

Along with many aristocrats of the time who feared a Catholic renaissance during the reign of James II, he became an active supporter of the Whig party and of the Protestant William of Orange and his wife Princess Mary, daughter of James II. He mobilized troops in the Midlands to support the Royal couple

BELOW LEFT *Diana Bruce, Countess of Rutland,* circle of Sir Peter Lely. She was the 9th Earl of Rutland's second wife. BELOW RIGHT *Catherine Noel, Countess of Rutland,* by Sir Godfrey Kneller. Catherine was the 9th Earl's third wife, and became the 1st Duchess of Rutland.

during their struggle for the throne before King James was deposed in 1689. He even sheltered Mary's sister, Princess Anne, at Belvoir when it became dangerous for her to live in London during the troubles of 1688.

Princess Anne became Queen Anne in 1702, and on 29 March 1703, after continued recommendation from Lady Russell (the Earl's son's mother-in-law), Queen Anne, 'in consideration of his great merits, and the services of his ancestors to the nation', bestowed two hereditary titles on the Earl, making him the 1st Duke of Rutland and the Marquis of Granby.

There was apparently some question as to which titles the 9th Earl would like to adopt. Rutland was readily accepted but the Lord Treasurer's suggestion of either Belvoir or Harborough for the Marquis did not seem to meet with the family's approval and, for a reason that is still not entirely clear, they chose the title the Marquis of Granby (and also opted for the French spelling of Marquis).

The 1st Duke died at Belvoir Castle in 1711 and was succeeded by his son John, who became the 2nd Duke of Rutland.

BELOW The Letters Patent from Queen Anne granting the dukedom to the family in 1703.
RIGHT *John Manners, 2nd Duke of Rutland*, by Jean-Baptiste Closterman.

THE 2ND DUKE OF RUTLAND, JOHN MANNERS, 1711–21

JOHN is perhaps unfairly remembered for being the pawn in his socially ambitious mother-in-law's schemes. Lady Russell was the mother of the Duke of Bedford and of the Duchess of Devonshire. She engineered the elevation of the Manners family from earls to dukes because she was not content with her daughter Katherine being merely a countess. Despite the obvious attractions of the Manners family's enormous wealth, the devoutly Christian Russells were concerned that John's father had been divorced and, quite simply, were only prepared for their daughter to marry

a Manners if she was eventually to become a duchess. That meant that her future father-in-law, the 9th Earl of Rutland, had to be made a duke. It took Lady Russell two attempts: the first, a begging letter to William III in 1702, probably fell on deaf ears – it was later found in the dead King's pocket; undeterred, she tried again a year later and persuaded Queen Anne to agree to her request, although it was said that the Queen did so with some reluctance.

Sadly, Katherine was duchess for only nine months: she died giving birth to her ninth child. Her bed, which she had commissioned using £500 that her father-in-law had given to her on the birth of her first son and heir, is one of the few prized pieces that remain in the castle from this period.

The 2nd Duke spent much of his time at the House of Lords: he was by then Lord Lieutenant of Leicester and was made a Knight of the Garter in 1714. He had eight more children by his second wife Lady Sherrard, daughter of the 2nd Baron Sherrard. Lady Russell, who with her husband had demanded so many conditions for their daughter on his first marriage, was fond of her son-in-law and, despite her grief at her daughter's death, had given him her blessing for his second marriage.

He died aged 44 of smallpox and was succeeded by his eldest son John, Marquis of Granby, who became the 3rd Duke of Rutland.

THE 3RD DUKE OF RUTLAND, JOHN MANNERS, 1721–79

'JOHN OF THE HILL', as he was affectionately known, was Duke of Rutland for 58 years, from 1721 to 1779. Like his father, he balanced the duties of his public life with the pleasures of country life and his own interests. He was a great patron of art with an intense interest in every detail of the practical process of painting. He became quite an accomplished painter himself, despite an infirmity in his hands that caused him so much pain when writing that he required permanent secretarial services – which were provided by Thomas Thoroton MP, a trusted and close friend of the Duke's son. He commissioned his portrait from the English artist Charles Jervas in 1725. He loved buying pictures at auctions and insisted on carrying his purchases home himself. 'No man', he said, 'deserved to have a good picture who would not carry it home.' Needless to say, many of them were quite small. He built a picture gallery in 1750 at Belvoir (with cellars underneath), but much of his collection has been sold over the years, including many pictures that he sold himself at Christie's in 1758 and 1761. He bought a particularly important painting by Poussin, *The Blind Orion Searching for the Sun*, in 1748, only to sell it again a few years later. Ironically, it was bought by Sir Joshua Reynolds, who later helped the Duke's grandson, the 4th Duke, to buy Poussin's famous *Sacraments* in 1786. (It is now in the Metropolitan Museum, New York.) The 3rd Duke's greatest legacy is the collection of Italian pictures that he began to buy in the 1740s: works by Shiadoni, Bassano, Carlo Dolci and Andrea del Sarto, all artists popular amongst English collectors in the 18th century.

The Duke also developed a rampant thirst for knowledge of the Classics. He employed the Earl of Oxford's tutor, the highly respected Michael Maittaire, who later went on to supervise the studies of Philip Stanhope, Lord Chesterfield's son. We don't know if he ever came to Belvoir but they began a correspondence which eventually amounted to four volumes of letters – many of which managed to include details of a day's hunting.

LEFT *John Manners, 3rd Duke of Rutland, 1725,* by Charles Jervas.
ABOVE *Bridget Sutton, 3rd Duchess of Rutland,* by Sir Godfrey Kneller.

Hunting featured heavily in the Duke's diary. He had a hunting lodge, Wilsford Hall, near Ancaster, Lincolnshire, and he built a new one: Croxton Park, in Leicestershire. In about 1730 the 3rd Duke and the Lords Gainsborough and Cardigan agreed to subscribe £300 each to a united hunt. Significantly, this was the first recorded pack in the Midlands. By formal agreement, the pack travelled to the estate of each contributor during the season. A few years afterwards the pack was divided into two units: one under the ownership of the Duke of Rutland, and the other under the ownership of the Earl of Gainsborough. It is from these packs that the Belvoir and Cottesmore Hunts are descended. The Belvoir Kennels have pack lists dating back to 1750.

ABOVE *Ordination, c.1637–40*, by Nicolas Poussin. On the advice of Sir Joshua Reynolds, the 4th Duke acquired the *Sacraments*, a series of seven pictures by the French artist Nicolas Poussin, in 1785, from the Bonapaduli family in Rome, amid enormous controversy. The Pope, who did not want them to leave Rome, had previously blocked their sale to Sir Robert Walpole. In great secrecy copies were made to hang in place of the originals before the originals could be smuggled out of the country. Reynolds, who was responsible for the cleaning and framing, declared 'Rome ... is now much poorer, as England is richer than it was, by this acquisition.' One of the series, *Penance*, was lost in the 1816 fire and another, *Baptism*, was sold to the National Gallery of Art, Washington, in 1939. The remaining five are now on loan to the National Gallery in London.

The Duke's interests and passions at home, as well as plans to build a new house in London, took their toll on Haddon Hall, which suffered dangerous blows of neglect. The 3rd Duke's family were the last to use it as an occasional residence; after that, it stood quietly dormant, slowly deteriorating, for nearly 200 years until the 9th Duke restored it.

The family acquired four manors – Averham, Kelham, Rolleston and Syerston in Nottinghamshire – when the Duke married Bridget Sutton, daughter and heiress of Lord Lexington, in 1717. An Act of Parliament was obtained in 1735 that allowed the Duke's younger sons and their respective sons to use the Sutton name. Of his 13 children only three boys survived: John, the famous soldier, the Marquis of Granby; Robert, who became Lord Robert Manners-Sutton, a celebrated naval officer, and lived at Kelham, in Nottinghamshire; and George,[14] who succeeded his unmarried brother Robert when Robert died aged 40.

Bridget died in 1734. Her husband was a widower for nearly 45 years but was comforted, in every way, by his late wife's lady's maid, 15-year-old Elizabeth Drake, from the neighbouring village of Woolsthorpe. The unconventional match developed into a full and loving relationship which lasted until his death in 1779. She was rather beautiful and a miniature of her, painted when she was only 16, is in the Picture Gallery. Adding to the unusualness of the set-up, her brother was the Duke's valet-de-chambre, a position he maintained with no apparent awkwardness long after his sister had assumed the role of châtelaine. His son and his sister's children dined together at Belvoir with the Duke and his mistress, while Mr Drake kept his place behind the Duke. For gossip-mongers the scandal was too juicy to ignore and *Town and Country Magazine* reported: 'There is indeed a whimsical hospitality that reigns throughout the family; while the menial servants are dwelling in plenty below stairs, the upper domestics are reclining in luxury in the offices and their master is assisting at the convivial board of the most elevated nobility, surrounded by bastards.'

The Duke and Elizabeth spent time at Belvoir and Haddon but they lived largely in Rutland House, a house they built on 7 acres of land on an 80-year-lease from an independent freehold estate in Knightsbridge, London. Despite all the tittle-tattle, the relationship was accepted and the Duke's heir, the Commander-in-Chief of land forces in Great Britain, the Marquis of Granby, was a regular visitor along with his wife, son and daughter-in-law (later the 4th Duke and Duchess of Rutland) and many military and political figures of the day.

The house, which cost just over £4,400 to build, was a mid-size Georgian mansion built of red brick and Portland stone, with a large garden, paddocks, orchard, conservatory, vinery, dairy, brew house and fowl houses. It had an unbroken view to Hyde Park, which was accessed by a private entrée awarded to the Duke from George II or III. When the 3rd Duke died in 1779 his son by Elizabeth, Edward Manners, paid the rates for her to carry on living in the house until her death in 1800.

The Duke had four children with Elizabeth Drake, two of whom survived: Roosilia (the name was derived from the Manners family name Roos or Ros), who was born in 1735, and Edward, in 1745. Their living arrangements were fascinating. Given that the castle was home to the Duke and his children from his late wife as well as to his mistress and their children, it is perhaps not surprising that a love-match occurred between one of the Manners children and one of the Thorotons, who were very close friends of the family. What is astonishing, and perhaps bears testament to the popularity of the Duke, is that it was the illegitimate Roosilia, whose surname (unlike her brother's) was registered as Drake, who married into the highly respectable Thoroton family when she married Thomas.

Thomas and Roosilia lived at the castle with their extended family and produced 13 children of their own, including John, who became Rector of Bottesford and private chaplain to the 4th and 5th Dukes, and is credited – with the 5th Duchess – with many of the plans for the rebuilding of the castle in which he had grown up as the 3rd Duke's grandchild. Keeping it in the family, so to speak, he in turn married his first cousin Elizabeth Manners, daughter of Roosilla's brother Edward, who lived in the rectory at nearby Goadby Marwood.

THE MARQUIS OF GRANBY,
JOHN MANNERS (b.1721 d.1770)

THE MARQUIS OF GRANBY, the 3rd Duke's eldest son, died before he succeeded to the title. During his lifetime he became one of the most famous men in England, and is probably the best known of all the family members who have lived at Belvoir. His title and portrait – hanging on signs outside public houses throughout the land – continue to keep his name in the public imagination.

> There was a time when Granby's grenadiers
> Trimm'd the lac'd jackets of the French Mounseers;
> And every week proclaimed some lucky hint,
> And all our paragraphs were planned by Pitt.[15]

He was an enormously popular national military hero, a soldier revered for his gallantry and humanity during the Seven Years War. It was said that during the reign of George III he was as popular as Nelson. With his high standards and integrity, he both inspired his troops before battles and supported them afterwards, particularly those who were invalided out of the army. He provided funds to help them set up businesses, many in the public houses which then bore his name: the Marquis of Granby. His generosity, however, cost him dear and when he died, he left debts of over £60,000.

His portrait was painted many times by Sir Joshua Reynolds and, unusually for the time, he is shown wearing neither a hat nor a wig, which was how he preferred to be seen. The story goes that as he led the British Cavalry in a splendid charge at the Battle of Warburg in 1760, his three-cornered hat came off. Ignoring the incident, the gallant Marquis dashed bald-headed into battle. The troops claimed they found it easier to follow him when the sun shone on his bald pate so he never covered his head again, which is where the saying 'to go bald-headed at ...' comes from, meaning to attack with great energy.

The Marquis's family assets, if not his cash-flow, increased considerably when he married Lady Frances Seymour, eldest daughter and co-heir of the Duke of Somerset. Cheveley Park, near Newmarket, was part of her dowry and the Manners would be grateful for it both as a

home and as a valuable source of cash and furniture when it was sold over a hundred years later.

Like his father and most of his other ancestors, the Marquis loved hunting and spent many a night at their hunting lodges, Wilsford Hall and Croxton Park. Fox hunting was becoming more established as a sport, moving from 'the legitimate slaughter of a noxious vermin to the carefully-regulated hunting of privileged beast of chase'. These are the words of T. F. Dale, historian of the Belvoir Hunt, who added: 'The Marquis of Granby was one of the first of a long line of English soldiers, statesmen, and judges

ABOVE A detail from *Cheveley Park*, 1671, by Jan Siberechts. This house was part of the dowry that Lady Frances Seymour brought to the family when she married the Marquis of Granby in 1750.
RIGHT *The Marquis of Granby*, by Sir Joshua Reynolds. He is seen in his uniform, leaniong on a mortar, with a battle in progress in the background.

whom the chase of the fox has helped to form.' The Marquis certainly knew his country and his hounds and he had a natural eye for hunting that many believed improved his mental approach to his soldiering. Another of his passions was booze and, 'like his son after him, Lord Granby was a convivial soul, and he flinched no more from the bottle than he did from foe'.[16]

Another interest that he shared with his father and his son was art. He patronized a number of the finest artists of the day, not least because many artists, including Alan Ramsey and the distinguished Swiss pastelist Jean-Etienne

Liotard, who visited London between 1748 and 1754, were keen to take the likeness of such a famous man. Liotard's half-length portrait of Lord Granby's father, the 3rd Duke, in oil – a rare medium for this artist – is particularly fine. It shows him wearing the Order of the Garter across his chest, his hat under his arm and clutching his chamois leather gloves.

Lord Granby's son, Lord Ros, succeeded to the courtesy title of the Marquis of Granby when his father died; and when his grandfather, the 3rd Duke (known by then as the Old Man of the Hill[17]), died he succeeded to the dukedom, becoming the 4th Duke of Rutland in 1779.

THE 4TH DUKE OF RUTLAND, CHARLES MANNERS 1779–87

THE 4TH DUKE was a duke for nine years and combined his considerable public duties, including his appointment as Lord Lieutenant of Ireland, with pleasurable pursuits. Like his father and grandfather, he was passionate about the arts and was elected Associate of the Royal Academy of Art in 1770. He was a patron and great friend of Joshua Reynolds, one of the most respected and influential painters of the 18th century. As well as painting many family portraits for the Duke during his regular visits to Belvoir, Reynolds advised him on buying pictures from other artists. He intervened during the contentious process of obtaining the series of paintings by Poussin, *The Sacraments*, from Rome for £2,000 in 1784 and also a portrait of Henry VIII believed to be by Holbein for 200 guineas in 1787.

But the 4th Duke's extravagant spending on art, his gambling, the expenses of public life and the enormous debts that he inherited from his father were leaving gaping holes in the cash-flow of the estate and, with little maintenance, the fabric of the castle itself was fast falling into disrepair. Lancelot 'Capability' Brown was commissioned to draw up plans for a new castle in 1780, which he did, giving it his trademark parkland setting, but there just wasn't enough money to proceed. Haddon Hall had been abandoned completely; the furniture was stored away in an unguarded barn, with the consequence that

LEFT *Lady Mary Isabella Somerset*, 1799, by Robert Smirke. Lady Mary was the daughter of the 4th Duke of Beaufort and married the 4th Duke of Rutland. Robert Smirke was commissioned to copy the original portrait at Badminton, Somerset, when Belvoir's portrait of the Duchess was burnt in the 1816 fire.

RIGHT *Charles Manners, 4th Duke of Rutland*, by Sir Joshua Reynolds.

much of it was stolen. Between 1776 and 1784 the family spent increasingly more time at his mother's former home, Cheveley Park.

The 4th Duke had married Lady Mary Isabella Somerset, daughter of the 4th Duke of Beaufort, who was known as the 'beautiful Duchess'. Sir Nathaniel Wraxhall wrote of her in his memoirs: 'It is not sufficient merely to say that she was the most beautiful woman in the kingdom of high rank. Her person, in symmetry, elegance and dignity outstripped all rivalry.'[18] She was painted three times by Reynolds, and immortalised in a poem in 1826 by George Crabbe, the Duke's former chaplain.[19]

> ... It was her smile that on each object shed
> Beauty and Grace and they with that are fled;
> She is not there, but all that here can be,
> Her love, her worth, her virtue dwell with thee;
> And all she once esteemed, admired, approved,
> Are doubly valued and as hers are loved.

Rather amusingly, she was also known later, after she had lost her looks, as 'Duchess Was-a-bella'. There is a wonderful story that a local woman had to forfeit her front tooth to replace one lost by the Duchess. Thank goodness for modern cosmetics and dentistry.

Among the Duke's many public offices, it was as Lord Lieutenant of Ireland that he was most popular and best remembered. His appointment in 1784 came just a few months after he had been made Lord Privy Seal by his close university friend and political ally William Pitt (the Younger), who had recently become Prime Minister. The Duke achieved measured success in Ireland but these achievements were recognized by both Parliament and the King. A letter to the Duke from Daniel Pulteney MP, on 27 January 1787, reads: 'a constituent tells me it is the opinion of the borough at Bramber that you are so liked in Ireland that the King cannot let you come home any more.' He added, tantalizingly, 'From a supposed resemblance to the Duchess of Rutland, added to her singing, Mrs Billington is making the town distracted.'

The Duke's affairs were well known: Elizabeth Billington was an opera singer who shared his attentions with those of Reynolds and the composer Haydn. He was also a regular client of Mrs Leeson at her brothel in Pitt Street, and one day allegedly spent 16 uninterrupted hours with her from one o'clock in the morning until five o'clock the following afternoon, while two of his aides-de-camp, on horses and armed with swords, remained outside.[20]

The lifestyle of the Lord Lieutenant of Ireland, with its obligatory extravagant entertaining of dignitaries, eminently suited the Duke. He had been warned, when he accepted the office with a £20,000 salary, that he would be expected to spend £15,000 of his own money annually to cover his expenses. The crippling costs necessitated him to write to his wife at Belvoir telling her cash was drying up fast. He asked her to be prudent with her household purchases and to avoid unnecessary expense on her own and the family's clothing, thus allowing him to continue his official duties in the manner to which he had become accustomed.

It wasn't just his finances that courted disaster: his limitless appetite for rich food and his voracious drinking habits were causing huge concern too. His sister wrote to

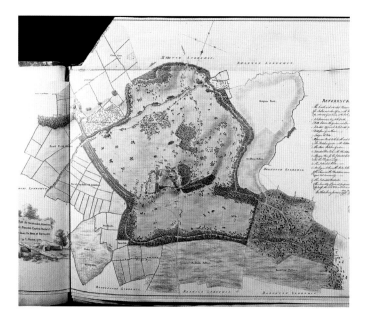

Lancelot 'Capability' Brown was commissioned to make plans for the park as well as the castle by the 4th Duke in the 1780s, but nothing was done until Elizabeth, the 5th Duchess, arrived at Belvoir in the early 1800s. She eventually carried out his landscaping proposals (top); the results are best seen from the roof of the castle (right).

Brown made detailed drawings of the third castle and the changes that he suggested are marked faintly in red (centre). His ideas, however, were not nearly grand or romantic enough for Elizabeth, and she took on James Wyatt to make much more radical alterations (bottom). For many generations it was thought that Elizabeth had razed the old house to the ground before building her neo-castle; the discovery of both Brown's and Wyatt's plans in the archives proved the contrary.

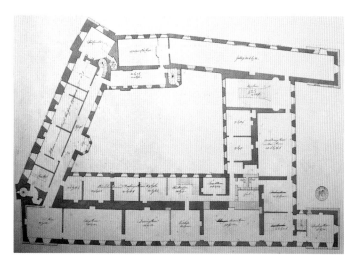

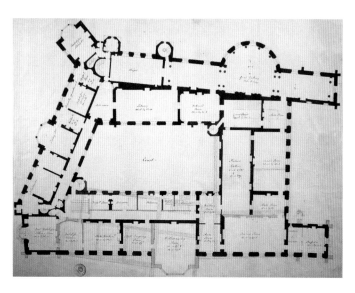

him on Christmas Day in 1784: 'the life your Grace leads is far too irregular for it to be possible for you to live long, much less in the chance of continuing in health.' She continued, rather prophetically: 'you used to tell me that the faculty was of opinion that your constitution was far from strong, and that it had been represented to you the necessity of being abstemious both in eating as well as *drinking*. Would to heaven that I could say any thing to influence you to take care of yourself! Health takes a sudden flight, and death happens unexpectedly.' Within three years her fears were justified. His gluttony was a beast too big to slay and his heavy consumption of claret led to the alcohol poisoning that killed him in 1787, aged only 34.

Despite the shock of his death and the financial difficulties it brought in its wake, it was apparent that he was held in high esteem: the funeral procession bringing his remains back from Dublin to the family mausoleum at Bottesford was met by many hundreds of mourners who had turned out along the route to pay their respects. The body lay in state overnight in a large room at the Blackmoors Head Inn, Nottingham, and the following day the cortège completed its journey with great pomp.

The 4th Duke left a wife and five children, and his eldest son John was only nine years old when he became the 5th Duke of Rutland. It is to the 5th Duke's wife, Elizabeth, that we owe the Belvoir that you see today – the fourth castle.

The Fourth Castle

from 1801

THE 5TH DUKE OF RUTLAND, JOHN HENRY MANNERS 1787–1857

I HAVE ALREADY OUTLINED the story of how Elizabeth, the 5th Duchess, appalled at the house she found as a young bride at Belvoir, set out on her plans for a new, romantic palace in her own style (see pages 10–13). Less than two years after she first arrived there, building work began, on Good Friday in 1801. During the years that followed, Wyatt's architectural genius, responsible for the extra storeys, projecting turrets and towers, huge three-storey bow window that was added to the Gallery and loggia that was added in front of the Chapel, began to satisfy Elizabeth's dreams. The project was an enormous undertaking, but Elizabeth seemed undaunted, and kept a keen eye on progress. From the profits of agriculture and his Derbyshire and Nottinghamshire coal mines, the Duke was able to finance the works (which included the building of a 2-mile-long tramline, from Muston Wharf on the Grantham Canal, to bring coal straight from the Duke's coalfields near Ilkeston to the coal cellars at Belvoir via the River Trent). The Duke admired what Elizabeth was doing and remained closely involved, even accompanying her on a shopping trip to Paris, specifically to buy things for the house, in 1814. She, in turn, greatly valued his opinions.

The fourth castle was nearing completion when, in September 1813, the first of two tragedies struck: James Wyatt was fatally injured in a road accident. His carriage had collided with a horse and cart on his way to London from another of his projects, Dodington Park in Gloucestershire. He was killed instantly. His loss at Belvoir

was cushioned only by the sterling support of the Revd John Thoroton and of Wyatt's three gifted sons, Benjamin, Philip and Matthew, who were able to continue where their father had left off. (Belvoir was the only house on which all four members of the family worked.)

By the New-Year period of 1813–14, the house was ready for a visit from the Prince Regent and his brother, the Duke of York, who later expressed their admiration for all that Wyatt and Elizabeth had achieved. The Long Gallery, used to receive the Royal party and to celebrate the Duke's 36th birthday and the christening of his eldest son, the Marquis of Granby,[21] was decorated for the occasion and renamed the Regent's Gallery by the Royal visitor. The adjacent new Round Tower was also elevated in status and became the Regent's Tower. The Revd John Thoroton was knighted in recognition of his design contributions and as director of the entire project. But, three years later, before the full outline of her Valhalla was to pierce the skyline so magnificently, the second tragedy unfolded. It would take Elizabeth the rest of her life to rectify.

In the early hours of the morning on 26 October 1816 fire tore unremittingly through the old part of the castle (the north-east and north-west wings), the new Entrance Hall, which was just being finished, the Grand Staircase (which disintegrated in the furnace) and the new Picture Gallery. Legend has it that it was only the immediate bricking-up of the entrance to the Regent's Gallery that prevented the inferno from spreading further. The gold plate melted in the Chapel and every pane of glass was broken. Building work costing £120,000, 115 pictures by artists including Titian, Rubens, Van Dyck and Reynolds, and a portrait of William Shakespeare, went up in smoke. Adding to the troubles and to Elizabeth's great frustration, much of the furniture that hadn't burnt was unnecessarily thrown out of the windows in all the panic and confusion. *The Times* reported: 'Great was the eagerness of the tenantry to preserve the furniture, and all attention to its safe removal was disregarded: pictures, cabinets, statues, velvet hanging and tapestry with every description of costly and magnificent decoration were thrown out of the windows and scattered on the lawn.' One of my father-in-law's favourite stories about the fire was how many of the treasures thrown from the embers and looted by the locals began to be recognized in neighbours' houses many generations later. When it seemed as though things could not get any worse, it was discovered that very little of the building and contents was properly insured. The great saving grace, however, was the survival of the Duke and Duchess's four children and new baby, Charles (later the 6th Duke), who were rescued by Sir John Thoroton because

LEFT *John Henry Manners, 5th Duke of Rutland, c.1794–6*, by John Hoppner.
RIGHT Isaac Cruikshank's caricature of the 5th Duke's seemingly debauched two-week-long coming-of-age house party in 1799. The celebrations allegedly cost £60,000 and were attended by the Prince of Wales. My favourite line of the cartoon is spoken by the dishevelled drunken man propositioning a fat cook in the fifth tableau: 'Shew me to bed – or give me something to drink – great lump of loveliness! – devine Cherry-bum; – hear me! – give me some drink, thou mighty Castle Spectre!'

THE HUMOURS of BELVOIR CASTLE—or the MORNING AFTER.

their parents were at Cheveley Park.[22] Elizabeth wrote to Sir John Thoroton, 'My poor Dear Sir John, I have felt for you more than I am able to express, in the late dreadful and lamentable event, and I assure you I feel so very very grateful for the great care you took of my poor Dear Children, and altho' I cannot help regretting the loss of the Pictures, and the beautiful Picture Gallery, all that appears nothing in comparison.'

The investigation that followed identified two places where the blaze had started. Rather shockingly, the fire was suspected to have been the work of arsonists: nine or ten intruders were seen leaving the castle as the initial alarm was raised. However, nothing was ever proved and the exact cause of the fire or motive for arson remains a mystery.

The Duke and Duchess were undeterred by the scale of the devastation and work resumed on 10 March 1817 to restore the damage and continue with the master plan. With Wyatt dead, Sir John Thoroton was in charge. His mettle would be tested at every turn and without pay. He once submitted an account for his services that so surprised Elizabeth that she wrote to her husband callously remarking, 'I always thought what he did was for his own amusement.' He withdrew his claim and never presented one again. Yet she could not have done without

him, and depended on him absolutely for the next phase of her building programme. She had three more babies after the fire; the pregnancies drained her mentally and physically and she spent a lot of time recovering at Cheveley. Sir John not only kept the show on the road but also made many valuable contributions of his own. He is credited with improvements in many of the rooms but principally with the overall design of the north entrance, the east front with the tower that houses the exquisite French-influenced Elizabeth Saloon, the replacement Grand Staircase, the Libraries, the Ballroom, the rebuilding of the State Dining Room and the general management of the Wyatt brothers, who worked on the interiors with Elizabeth. His death aged 62, just four years after the fire, was a bitter blow. Elizabeth wrote to her friend and adviser, the Irish MP Colonel Frederick Trench, with whom she shared many of her creative ideas: 'I wander about ... crying all the way I go, for everything I see recalls him to my imagination.'[23]

Two years later, in 1818, it was the Duke who was writing to Trench; in his letter he implies that he was aware that his adored wife was having an affair with the universally popular Duke of York. There were suggestions circulating among her social circles that she had other lovers too[24] but

LEFT An oil painting based on an illustration from a local newspaper portrays the fire that destroyed so much of the castle in 1816. The picture was bought by my father-in-law in 1989.
RIGHT *Elizabeth, Duchess of Rutland*, by George Sanders. The painter reputedly put himself somewhere in the picture, presumably in the carriage. Sometime after the Duchess's death he returned to Belvoir Castle to add the finished castle, the lake and the bridge which had been completed in 1824.

the 59-year-old Duke of York, second son of George III, was clearly infatuated with the 42-year-old Elizabeth. A friend of the Rutlands, Harriet Arbuthnot, witnessed their behaviour at a dinner party and wrote in her diary in June 1825: 'The Duke is most absurdly & ridiculously in love with the Dss of Rutland.' A few weeks later she wrote: 'I went to dinner with the Duke of Rutland, and on the other side sat the Dss of Rutland & the Duke of York. He was engaged to dine at Mr. Robinson's, but neither went nor sent an excuse & was waited for till past 9 o'clock. He staid the whole day & ev'g with the Dss of Rutland, making himself more ridiculous than any thing I ever saw.'25

At her Royal lover's request, Elizabeth helped Benjamin Wyatt to design a new home for him in 1825: York (later Lancaster) House close to her own London address, Rutland House in Arlington Street. The Duke of York was oblivious to the expense. Costs, including Wyatt's building fees, soared to £120,000.

Her life at that time was happy and fulfilled. She was in her prime. She was occupied at home with finishing the interiors (chiefly the Elizabeth Saloon), running the estate and looking after her devoted family, involved with building projects further afield and enjoying her open relationship with the Duke of York. So the news of her sudden death on

29 November 1825, aged only 45, from a burst appendix, was met with crushing disbelief that sent distraught shockwaves across the country. A document was circulated from the castle that included the following passage: 'A disconsolate family will forever deplore her untimely death – a wide circle of friends will be deprived of its brightest ornament – and the country at large will have reason to regret the loss of that public spirit and those varied talents which were beginning to attract general attention.'

Elizabeth's death shook all those around her but her husband's grief was palpable. The Revd Irvin Eller, the Duke's chaplain, wrote of her funeral: 'The Duke evidently made an effort to repress his feelings, and for some time joined in the responses but ere half the ceremony was ended he closed the book, and gave way to uncontrolled emotion.'[26] Just days after her death the Duke wrote heart-rendingly to his mother (Mary Isabella, the Dowager Duchess): 'I fear

you will find the melancholy recollections and the gloomy appearances of this Castle are more than what you expect. The absence and want of the Beautiful Hand by which every thing with in the Castle and its neighbourhood was arranged and much enjoyed, are more & more felt & experienced; and I myself know from the experience of every hour, that the wretchedness and helplessness of my situation ... have not been exaggerated ...'

In the immediate aftermath of her death both the Duke of York and the Duke of Wellington visited Belvoir to comfort the widower. HRH stayed with the Duke for two weeks, their mutual tears pooling on the écarté table in the unfinished Elizabeth Saloon. It is difficult to understand how Elizabeth's grief-stricken husband managed to maintain any composure with his old friend and Royal rival. The letter to his mother suggests that behind the polite façade he was clearly struggling: 'The Duke of York arrived last night. He feels this dreadful affliction as he was there. To feel the loss of so kind and efficient a friend,' and continues, 'I wish him ill. He is going out shooting and I mean some other day to try and force myself out with him, but I have declined to-day.'

Only a month after Elizabeth's death Matthew Cotes Wyatt was back at work with 115 workmen, including joiners and gilders, to finish the Elizabeth Saloon.[27] He himself painted the ceiling to Elizabeth's designs, which featured mythological figures representing her family and friends including the Duke of York.

Elizabeth's death perhaps proved all too much for the Royal duke. After laying the first stone of her mausoleum at Belvoir,[28] in March 1826, he spent an hour by himself in the cold, damp vault that was to be her final resting place. He caught a chill which by May had taken full grasp of his already deteriorating health. In January 1827 'The Grand Old Duke of York' succumbed to dropsy and heart disease. He died in Elizabeth's London home, Rutland House, where he had spent the last four months of his life with the Duke of Rutland close by him.

The Duke resolved to finish his wife's castle which, after the fire, cost another £82,000 and took nearly five more years to complete. A proposed visit from Queen Victoria, Prince Albert and the Dowager Queen Adelaide (on her second visit) prompted some alterations of his own to suit the Royal party's convenience. He wrote to his son Lord Granby at Belvoir, a month before her visit, to confirm some proposals. 'Well! We have agreed your plan for a new Bed Stead altogether in the Chinese Bed Room, and it will be ready – and I perfectly agree to the private Drawing Room below stairs being fitted up for <u>my</u> Bed

Room . . . I shall be superbly lodged. The difficulty is about the Green Room which <u>cannot</u> in my opinion be given up as the Royal Sitting Room. The Elizabeth Saloon would be too large and stately . . . which I should like to sit there on one of the evenings . . . '

The Royals drew huge crowds when they arrived at Belvoir in December 1843 and also when they attended a meet of the Belvoir Hounds at Croxton Park. T. F. Dale recounted that 'The Queen and her Consort, Queen Adelaide (widow of William IV) and the Duke of Rutland

OPPOSITE LEFT *H.R.H. Frederick Augustus, Duke of York*, 1826, by Andrew Geddes. The Duke of York, the second son of George III, was a close, personal friend of the 5th Duchess of Rutland from about 1818 until her death in 1825.

OPPOSITE RIGHT A marble statue of Elizabeth reaching for heaven, by Matthew Cotes Wyatt, dominates the Mausoleum, which was built in her memory in 1826. Members of the Rutland family have been buried there ever since.

RIGHT *John Henry, 5th Duke of Rutland*, by George Sanders. He is seen wearing his robes for the coronation of George IV in 1820.

LEFT *The Melton Hunt Breakfast*, by Sir Francis Grant. This was painted for the 5th Duke at the request of W. Little Gilman Esq., who is seen seated in the armchair and surrounded by other key figures of the hunting fraternity. Melton Mowbray was the epicentre of hunting in Leicestershire in the 19th century and the area was home to numerous members of the aristocracy during the season. Hunting has been integral to the lives of all the Dukes of Rutland, including my late father-in-law who, as Master of Foxhounds, led the Belvoir Hunt for many years until the 1950s. This was one of his favourite pictures in the castle.

OPPOSITE BELOW *Hunting Scene near Belvoir Castle,* 1828, by John Ferneley. The 5th Duke is seen on his grey horse in the distance with his brothers Lieutenant General Lord Charles Manners on the left and Major General Lord Robert Manners in the foreground.

BELOW *Belvoir Castle,* 1814, by Thomas Wright, portrays the romantic quality that Elizabeth was so determined to achieve.

rode to the Meet in a carriage drawn by four horses and attended by outriders dressed in his Grace's livery', and continued, 'They were accompanied by hundreds of horsemen, and the route was lined for nearly a quarter of a mile by carriages of all descriptions. By the time the carriage reached the Park around 800 horsemen were present, including the Duke of Wellington, with thousands on foot. All present gave three cheers for the two Queens, before Prince Albert mounted his favourite hunter,

"Emancipation".'[29] The private route they took still exists and is known as the Carriage and Horses Drive as reminder of that momentous occasion.

The Duke's keen and continued interest in shooting kept him occupied for much of the winter. He would often spend most of the partridge season (from September to February) entertaining family and friends at Cheveley Park. Belvoir was the focus for extensive partying in the hunting season although the Duke lost interest in riding to hounds himself after Elizabeth's death. It is said that during the first four months of 1839, 1997 people dined at the Duke's table and another 11,312 within the castle.[30] No one staying at Belvoir could have missed the band (of the Leicestershire militia) playing martial music on the terrace every morning. (Nowadays guests wake up to the castle's rat-catcher playing the bagpipes.) His interest in racing, which was never strong, also waned after he was

widowed. Earlier in his life, encouraged by his friends the Duke of York, the Earl of Chatham and Mr Sloane Stanley, the Duke had somewhat reluctantly become a member of the Jockey Club, and his best horse, Cadland, won the Derby in 1828.

He was Lord Lieutenant of Leicestershire from 1799 until his death, was made Knight of the Garter in 1803 and was an active member of the House of Lords, notably speaking out against the repeal of the Corn Laws in the 1840s. He showed great admiration and support for his friend the Duke of Wellington and formed a committee to commemorate the national hero with a sculpture by Matthew Cotes Wyatt, which now stands above the Arch at the top of Constitution Hill.

In 1838, during one of the Duke's notorious birthday celebrations at Belvoir, Charles Greville, the political diarist, said of him: 'The Duke is as selfish a man – as any of his class, that is. He never does what he does not like, and spends his life in a round of such pleasures as suit his taste, but he is neither a foolish nor a bad man, and partly from a sense of duty, partly from inclination, he devotes time and labour on his estate.'[31]

The 5th Duke of Rutland died just over two weeks after his 79th birthday. Some members of the family would say his greatest achievement was encouraging his wife to build this splendid castle. Others would say that his greatest error was to indulge his wife in building a castle that stripped the family of a considerable fortune. On the whole, though, he was considered to be both fair and honest – qualities that his sons, the 6th and 7th Dukes of Rutland, inherited.

THE 6TH DUKE OF RUTLAND, CHARLES CECIL JOHN MANNERS 1857–88

THE MARQUIS OF GRANBY (Lord Granby, as he was known until he succeeded to the dukedom aged 42 in 1857) was a longed-for son and heir. His parents had been married for sixteen years before he was born and had already had seven children, including two boys who had died in infancy. His recently discovered letters and diaries reveal a man of great sensitivity who had a deep and loving relationship with his parental family, although he never married.

Having followed the family's traditional educational route – Eton and Trinity College, Cambridge, Lord Granby entered politics as Conservative MP for Stamford in 1837. He held his seat for 11 years until he moved to the North Leicestershire seat for a further five years. He was so clearly not cut out for politics that the length of his political life is remarkable.

In 1843, after Queen Victoria and Prince Albert had stayed at Belvoir, he was offered the office of Lord of the Bedchamber. Prince Albert, in a letter to Lord Granby's father, wrote: 'having at our last pleasant visit at Belvoir Castle made the acquaintance of your son Lord Granby, I should see with great pleasure, that by his acceptance of this place he were to be brought in nearer relation to me. I prefer to make communication to Your Grace presuming that Lord Granby would consult you before coming to a final decision.'

Granby got into a state of anxiety about this, writing to his father: 'the offer was so unexpected, to consider about it, and did not like therefore to state my objections too

strongly and moreover we had / after having stated them / to leave it to your better judgement to decide.' He went on to explain how he felt unsuitable for the role and also admitted that politics was not for him either: 'I fear, I who know and care little for politics personally, and would rather live altogether a <u>retired</u> life; and be <u>out</u> of Parliament, am saying too much.' Nevertheless he did accept the office and served Prince Albert for three years.

Things got worse for him in his political career. In 1848, as a staunch protectionist,[32] he was elected leader of the Conservative Party after Lord George Bentinck's resignation. Charles Greville wrote in his diary, 'Except his high birth, he has not a single qualification for the post; he is tall, good looking, civil and good humoured, if these are qualifications, but he is heavy, dull and ignorant, without ability or knowledge, destitute of ideas to express and the art of expressing them if he had any; and yet this great party can find no better man.'[33] By his own admission Lord Granby felt inadequate; he was known to break down during debates, and resigned after only three weeks, leaving the party leaderless. At the beginning of the next parliamentary session in January 1849 he was persuaded to join Disraeli and John Charles Herries as a joint leader but

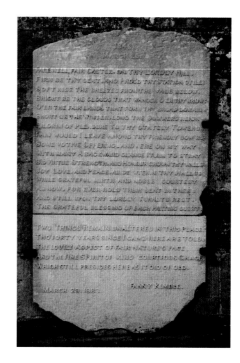

continued to feel uncomfortable and resigned again in 1852. He remained an MP, however, and continued his support for agricultural protectionism, some of his speeches even proving to be prophetic; and he succeeded his father as Lord Lieutenant for Leicestershire in 1857.

The Duke was happier out of limelight and much preferred to be at home, hunting, shooting and entertaining – he was a legendary host, or else at sea, sailing with friends. He was said to be one of the most popular Masters of Hounds that had ever existed. The family's hunting box at Wilsford Hall, near Sleaford, had been sold in 1815 and Croxton Park was occupied by the widow of huntsman Will Goodall, so he built himself a new lodge at Knipton. This is now our hotel and restaurant: The Manners Arms.

His quiet respect while out hunting was contrasted by fairly rowdy entertaining afterwards, his trademark cigar – which Lord Wilton christened 'bowsprits' – always close to hand. He hosted huge house parties at Belvoir during the hunting season and for the popular Croxton Park Races at Easter. A great many leading members of society, including the Prince of Wales, who stayed twice, passed through Belvoir's doors over the years. Christmas was also particularly well celebrated: records for 1860 show that 30 members of his family stayed for the week-long festivities;

they were looked after by some 200 members of his own staff and a further 300 brought by his guests.

He inherited his passion for sailing from his father and shared it with his brothers. Regattas at Cowes and Rye were a big feature during their summers, and they won many trophies over 24 years with their yacht, a schooner named *Resolution*. It was replaced in 1869 with *Shark*, another schooner which, after it had been lengthened by 8 feet to 108 feet, was used for cruising. She too was replaced in 1885 with a larger ketch, *Lufra*.

Charles remained a bachelor all his life, despite being highly eligible and exceptionally handsome. It may be that he never found anyone to compare to the first woman he loved and wanted to marry: Selina Forester.[34] She was his first cousin, but his father disapproved of the match and they were forbidden to marry. The entries in his diary that lead up to her wedding to Sir Orlando Bridgeman (later 3rd Earl of Bradford) are increasingly desperate. On 11 April 1844 it reads: 'Hunted at 6 in the morning at Croxton Park. S. Forester, Tomlyn and I – for the last time?' The following day: 'Came to town with S.F. I am like a person in a dream. Everything seems confused but there is this sad difference, the dreamer believes what is not true, whereas I can't believe what is true.' The entry for 30 April, the day of

her wedding, is boxed in thick ink and reads: 'Tuesday –
contentedness and not happiness is now all I seek.' The
heavily inked sketches of her with which he illustrated
some of the pages demonstrated his turmoil and agony, but
also show him to be an accomplished artist.

Nevertheless, he was later described as rather roguish.
Writing in her book *My Recollections*, Lady Cardigan, a
childhood friend and frequent visitor to Belvoir, says,
'Lord Granby was a man of consummate tact and presence
of mind. At one of his houseparties there was a pretty
young married lady with whom he was greatly smitten,
and having received every encouragement, he paid a visit to
her room after she had retired. The lady was asleep, and just
as the Marquis was about to rouse her, the door opened,
and the husband, whom he supposed to be otherwise
engaged, appeared unexpectedly on the scene. It was an
embarrassing moment, but the Marquis, who was equal to
the occasion, held up a warning finger and exclaimed in an
anxious whisper, "Hush! Don't disturb her, she is fast
asleep; I was passing, and I thought I smelt fire – but all's
well." The husband thanked him with honest gratitude.'[35]

Fanny Kemble, the actress, was a guest at Belvoir. She had
also been a friend of the 5th Duchess and it has been
suggested that the habit of taking afternoon tea was
invented during one of her visits to see Elizabeth. One
afternoon, a fellow guest, the Duchess of Bedford, allegedly
requested a light snack and a cup of tea to stave off hunger
pangs – and the tradition began. Staying with the Duke a
few years before his death, Fanny wrote the following verse:

> Two things remain unaltered in this place
> The forty years since I came here are told
> The lovely aspect of fair nature's face
> And the fine spirit of kind courteous grace
> Which still presides here as it did of old.

This is as fine a testament to Elizabeth as it is to her son.

The 6th Duke continued hunting into his late 60s, when
gout and injuries from a particularly bad fall forced him to
stop; and he carried on shooting to within weeks of his
death. He died in 1888 aged 73, after a long and painful
illness. His brother, Lord John Manners, succeeded to the
dukedom aged 70.

OPPOSITE LEFT The pitiful state of mind of the Marquis of
Granby (later the 6th Duke) in the days leading up to the
wedding of his beloved cousin Selina Forester is clearly revealed
in his diary. He had wanted to marry Selina but was forbidden to
do so by his father.

OPPOSITE RIGHT Fanny Kemble was a friend of the 5th Duchess
as well as of the 6th Duke. She wrote the first of these two poems
about Belvoir in 1842 and the second over 40 years later in 1883.
The terrace is a fitting place for her testaments to the beauty of
the place as it one of the first things that visitors see at Belvoir.

BELOW *Charles Manners, 6th Duke of Rutland*, by Sir Francis Grant.
The Duke is seen in the robes of the Order of the Garter.

LEFT *Catherine Marlay, Lady John Manners,* by Richard Buckner. Catherine was the first wife of Lord John Manners, later 7th Duke of Rutland. She died in 1854 giving birth to her second child, and left a devastated young husband and a two-year-old son, Henry, later the 8th Duke. Her beauty is so delicate and there is a vulnerability about her that I find quite breathtaking.

OPPOSITE ABOVE *John Manners, 7th Duke of Rutland,* English School.

OPPOSITE BELOW *Janetta, Duchess of Rutland,* 1891, English School. Janetta was the 7th Duke's second wife and appears robust in comparison to his fragile-looking first wife, Catherine; but Janetta died in1899, leaving him a grieving widower again.

THE 7TH DUKE OF RUTLAND,
JOHN JAMES ROBERT MANNERS, 1888–1906

WE HAVE TWO WRITERS, Lady Diana Cooper, grand-daughter of the 7th Duke, and Charles Whibley, who wrote Lord John's political biography in 1925, to thank for much of what we understand about the life of the 7th Duke.

Diana had only fond memories of her grandfather. Visits to his 'ugly house' in Cambridge Gate in London were contrasted to many of her childhood winters spent at Belvoir for the hunting. By then he was in his eighties and must have seemed very old to the young adolescent. The old-fashioned ways of doing things at the castle must have been fascinating to an enquiring mind. She wrote, 'Lord John (now the Duke) was a beautiful bent old man. I can see him very clearly, walking down the endless corridors of Belvoir, wrapped warmly in a thick black cape buttoned down the front, for these passages in winter were arctic – no stoves, no hot pipes, no heating at all. He would unbutton his cape at the drawing room door and hang it on a long brass bar with many others ... I would sit on his bony knees when the meal was over, and be allowed to blow open his gold hunter watch, and ask for a comical poem that he and I both liked to hear recited in a singsong tone ...'[36] The assembly of domestics with specific tasks left a life-long impression on her. Separate from the usual household staff, they included the long-white-bearded man who rang the gong three times a day, the lamp-and-candle-men (gas was considered vulgar), the coal man, the giant-like water men in brown clothes carrying two pails of water from yokes on their shoulders and the nocturnal watchmen padding round the corridors and terraces, silent but for their cries of 'Past twelve o'clock. All's well.'

Diana said the only drawback to staying at Belvoir was the need to be polite to some of the eccentric aunts and uncles who lived there. Her father Henry, later the 8th Duke, was the only child of his father's first marriage to the beautiful Catherine Marlay; she died in 1854 giving birth to her second baby, who also died. Eight years passed before he married again, this time the not-so-beautiful Janetta Hughan. All eight of Henry's half brothers and sisters met rather tragic ends. Edward died of tuberculosis aged 39. Cecil threw himself under a train aged 80. Bobby,

revive their traditional, paternal role and protect the working classes from industrial exploitation by middle-class businessmen. Gladstone described him at the time as 'an excellent candidate, a popular and effective speaker, and a good canvasser by virtue of his kindly disposition.'[37]

One of Young England's founding members was the statesman and novelist Benjamin Disraeli, who remained a close friend and political ally of the Duke for 40 years. Disraeli described the Duke in a letter to Queen Victoria as: 'a statesman with a large practical experience of public affairs, a student as well as a practical statesman; thoroughly versed in all the great political questions of Eastern and European politics; an admirable administrator with a great capacity of labour; a facile pen; a brave, firm and thorough gentleman'.[38] In Disraeli's political novel *Coningsby*, the character of Lord Henry Sidney is based on Lord John.

Lord John himself had literary aspirations, penning the controversial *England's Trusts and other Poems*, which he dedicated to another great friend, colleague and Young Englander, George Smythe, whom he had met at Cambridge University. An unfortunate couplet from the *England's Trust* poem, 'Let wealth and commerce, laws and learning die, / But leave us still our old nobility', caused enough ridicule to haunt him for the rest of his life. Other works of his were published, including *A Cruise in Scotch Waters on Board the Duke of Rutland's Yacht 'Resolution'*, illustrated by John Christian Schetky, in 1848; *Notes of an Irish Tour* in 1849; and another volume of patriotic poetry, *English Ballads and other Poems,* in 1850.

While staying with friends in Yorkshire during the summer of 1850, he had the good fortune to meet the already celebrated Charlotte Brontë at her home in Haworth. Writing to his brother Granby, he said: 'She is very shy and retiring, but after a short delay came into the room: pale, thin, pretty manners, very intelligent countenance. A drawing of her by Richmond hung on the wall, rather like her, but far more like "Becky Sharp" in "Vanity Fair"... Her father is a tipsy old Tory parson.' Lord John was well received, as he had had the foresight to take them a brace of grouse – for which her father apparently had a particular taste.

In 1850, at the age of 32, Lord John took his place for the first time in government, as Lord Derby's First

a hero in the Boer War and Master of the Belvoir Hounds, distinguishable by his eyeglass and long drawl, died aged 45 in the First World War. (His widow Mildred lived on at the Knipton hunting lodge built by the 6th Duke until her death in 1934.) William died aged 24 of unknown causes. Francis died in infancy in 1875. Kitty, aged 34, jumped off the bridge into the lake with all her jewellery on, holding aloft a parasol. Queenie never married and had to look after her father after her mother died in 1899. Elsie married Lord George Scott but died young.

The 7th Duke had a political career that spanned over half a century and, outside his family circle, was respected as a British statesman. In the early 1840s, as an MP for Newark (along with William Gladstone), he was a leading member of the Young England political group that encouraged aristocrats, landowners and the church to

Commissioner of Works. Some of his many duties included organizing the placement of the lions in Trafalgar Square, sorting out the controversy surrounding the future use of the Crystal Palace built for the 1851 Great Exhibition and arranging the ceremony for the Duke of Wellington's funeral. By 1874 he was Postmaster-General for Disraeli and was again for Lord Salisbury from 1885 to 1886, after which he was Chancellor of the Duchy of Lancaster until Salisbury's government left office in 1892. That year Queen Victoria wrote in her journal: 'saw the Duke of Rutland (who had succeeded his brother), who will not, I fear, be able to take office again. He is so kind and amiable, such a perfect gentleman, and a grand seigneur, that I shall miss him very much.'

The Queen was right: he did not hold office again, but his politics remained steadfast to the end. He had been forced to sell Cheveley Park in 1893, which he blamed on 'the injurious consequences of a system of free trade'. (It is likely that it was becoming a financial burden anyway.) Charles Whibley wrote of him in his retirement: 'At last he was able to realise in himself and in his surroundings the gospel of Young England. Far from the grasping democracy which construes benefits for rights, he still stood firm in the ways of feudalism.'[39]

In 1862 he had built a house, St Mary's Tower, near Birnam in Perthshire (now demolished), where he spent many holidays and to which he returned regularly in his retirement. (The pre-Raphaelite painter John Everett Millais rented it from him in 1874 and painted *The Fringe of the Moor* while he was there.) The Duke's last years were spent in quiet reflection at Belvoir mourning the death of his second wife Janetta, with his memories, his writing and his books. One of his last public engagements was as a pall-bearer at William Gladstone's funeral in 1898. He died in August 1906 aged 88 and Henry John Brinsley, his eldest son from his first marriage, succeeded to the dukedom.

OPPOSITE The family installed the memorial window to Janetta, the 7th Duke's second wife, in the south transept of Bottesford Church in 1902.
RIGHT *Henry Manners, 8th Duke of Rutland*, 1895, by Sir James Jebusa Shannon.

THE 8TH DUKE OF RUTLAND, HENRY JOHN MANNERS, 1906–25

HENRY WAS 54, good looking and 6 feet 2 inches tall when he became the 8th Duke of Rutland. He was married with three children, one of whom, Diana, was presumed to be the daughter of her mother's lover, Harry Cust; another, Lord Haddon, had died aged nine. Working life, as an MP for Melton Mowbray and principal private secretary to the

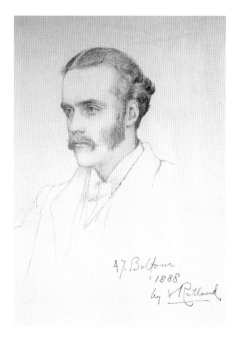

Marquess of Salisbury when Salisbury was Prime Minister, took him to Westminster where he was nicknamed 'Lord Salisbury's Manners'.

His early married life was probably happy but the conjugal relationship broke down after only a few years. He was unambitious, fairly anti-social and capable of terrible temper tantrums – he once ferociously threw all the breakfast plates on the floor when he heard that Princess Beatrice of Battenberg was coming for lunch. He sought comfort in the seductive charms of London's actresses, fathering a child by his 'favourite', Violet Vanbrugh. Lord Beaverbrook described him, rather unfairly one might hope, during a conversation with his daughter Diana one evening as 'a man of considerable stupidity'. His life as an English nobleman was reasonably predictable; his wife's was certainly not.

The 8th Duchess, Violet, was a great beauty, and one of the original Souls. These were an informal group of aristocratic politicians, intellectuals and artists who, from the 1870s to the turn of the century, preferred to talk about their souls rather than about politics. Violet had an impressive artistic talent which she channelled into hundreds of drawings, many of which now hang on the castle walls. Her finest work was the sculpture of her dead son, Lord Haddon, painstakingly worked on over several months in a London studio while she attempted to deal with her overwhelming grief. A finished plaster cast was exhibited at the Tate Gallery before it came to the Chapel at Belvoir, and a marble copy was made for the chapel at Haddon Hall.

While the 7th Duke was alive, the family lived first at 23a Bruton Street in London and a house in Bedfordshire (rented, rather boldly, from the Brownlows, relations of Violet's lover Harry Cust), and then, after Janetta, the 7th Duke's second wife, died in 1899, they moved into Rutland House at 16

OPPOSITE *Violet, Duchess of Rutland*, 1890, by Sir James Jebusa Shannon. She would only ever be portrayed in profile.
ABOVE Drawings by Violet, from left to right: The Prince of Wales; the actress Miss Gertrude Lawrence; Arthur Balfour, politician and statesman, who was Chief Secretary for Ireland at the time he sat for Violet. Violet's daughter Diana described her work as 'etherealising her sitters with her skilled pencil'.

Portraits of three children of the 8th Duke and Duchess by Sir James Jebusa Shannon. Clockwise, from below: John, later 9th Duke of Rutland, *c.*1898–9; Marjorie, later Marchioness of Anglesey, 1906; and Diana, later the wife of Duff Cooper, 1st Viscount Norwich, 1919.

ABOVE LEFT Violet, the 8th Duchess, with Marjorie, Lord Haddon and Violet, known as Letty.

ABOVE RIGHT Violet with Lord Haddon.

LEFT Violet holding Letty, with Lord Haddon and Marjorie.

BELOW Lord John, later the 9th Duke, as a young boy at Belvoir.

Arlington Street in London. Violet spent her mornings in bed writing letters and the afternoons drawing portraits. Her subjects included leading politicians, actors and actresses and, on one occasion, Queen Victoria. According to her daughter Diana their family existence was idyllic.

Everything changed when Henry succeeded to the dukedom when his father died in 1906: Belvoir became home and Violet began modernizing at once. Bathrooms were added, a telephone was put in, heating was installed, the old retainers – watchmen, gong-man, lamp-and-candle-men and water men – were considered no longer necessary and a motorcar (a Renault) was bought. The car is still here in good working order and spends most of its time being admired in the Portico. Christmas was still celebrated to the full: hordes of staff would be on duty, all the finest plate and silver were brought out and hundreds of real candles were lit on the Christmas tree.

The youngest children (now teenagers) adapted well to their new surroundings and enjoyed acting as castle guides giving rather ad-lib tours to unsuspecting visitors. Violet embraced the changes with vigour and used her artistic abilities to great effect in the alterations she made at Belvoir, all of which she recorded in a

notebook. Her husband, however, seemed distant and detached from his new life.

Diana adored the Duke but wrote: 'My father was frankly philistine. He was wise and knew about dry-fly fishing and how to be loved, but very little about the possessions which he inherited late in life.'[40] The house had welcomed visitors since it was built and the 7th Duke had revelled in the interest that they showed, but his son, an occasional guide, took a casual approach. 'With a gesture', wrote Diana, 'he would wave a whole wall away – a wall studded with the finest Nicholas Hilliard miniatures – with a: "Don't worry about those: they're all fakes."'[41]

Violet was a free spirit: she didn't approve of punishment or formal education for her girls but did expect them to learn poetry, the piano and about history and art, especially Pre-Raphaelite art, of which she was a great fan. She brought up the girls liberally, even by bohemian standards, and encouraged them to accept walk-on parts in some of the theatrical productions of her friend Sir Herbert Beerbohm Tree. Her surviving son John was, of course, sent to Eton. Although she had a calm disposition, Violet seldom showed signs of real emotion and, by all accounts, had a minimal sense of humour. She was also a terrible snob: she believed that a great many things, including tomatoes, were 'common'.

The onset of the First World War changed everything again. To Violet's credit, she converted Rutland House in London into an officers' hospital and had it kitted out to look after 22 patients, with an operating theatre in what was her bedroom. One of the nurses, Malony, stayed on with the family after the war; she looked after the Duke in his old age, and would wheel him around the terraces at Belvoir. The castle, too, was equipped to take patients and used as a convalescent home. Violet ran them both.

Diana took up nursing at Guy's Hospital, much to the pride of her father but to the distress of her mother, who feared she would be

remembers visiting her beloved grandmother in bed in the old Nursery, which is now our kitchen: apparently Violet had a revulsion for grey hair and would tuck it all in a cap and peer out over the bedcovers.

Aunt Ursie had fond memories of life at the castle when she was a young girl. She remembered Miss Felgate, Violet's maid, who was hunch-backed and a little lame, and Leena, the head housemaid, who was always very nice to her. 'I used to help the six housemaids to polish the floor in the Regent's Gallery: everyone would throw things at each other, it was a great lark. I remember there always seemed to be three boys on duckboards in the kitchen who were cleaning the copper pots. There was also a track on the floor in the Servants' Hall for beer to be trolleyed along it. And of course the footmen were always dressed in white tie.' Her grandfather's presence in the kitchen was not unheard of either and he was not unknown to throw loaves of bread at the baker if he considered that they were too hard to eat.

unable to cope. Letty nursed at Rutland House; John, despite a weak chest, enlisted in the 4th Battalion, the Leicestershire Regiment; and Marjorie stayed at home nursing her first child. There was a brief respite when John, by then a captain serving as an ADC to Sir John French, married Kathleen Tennant while he was on leave in 1916.

After the war, life at Belvoir slipped slowly back into its old routine. The Duke and Duchess remained somewhat at odds with one another and though the children had grown up, family life remained important and Belvoir provided the backdrop for a united family front. The introduction of death duties in 1894, however, had had a catastrophic effect on the estate. Like almost every other great estate in the country, Belvoir was forced to sell a huge percentage of its land to meet the demands for payment. In 1920, 13,300 acres of the Leicestershire estate were sold. (John had to take the decision to sell 44 pictures after he succeeded for the same reason.)

The 8th Duke died in 1925; Violet lived for another ten years. Aunt Ursie (Lady Ursula), my husband's aunt,

OPPOSITE When the 8th Duke inherited Belvoir in 1906, his wife Violet set about modernizing their home, installing electricity, heating and a telephone system.
ABOVE The 8th Duke's 1908 Renault car with Charles, the future 10th Duke of Rutland, in the driving seat with my husband's Aunt Isobel next to him, and Aunt Ursie in the back.
RIGHT *Henry Manners, 8th Duke of Rutland*, in the uniform of the Lord Lieutenant of Leicestershire, 1923, by Richard Jack.

THE 9TH DUKE OF RUTLAND,
JOHN HENRY MANNERS, 1925–40

IF EVER A SON could be more different from his father it was John. His only surviving son, Aunt Ursie's brother, Lord Roger Manners, described him as a charismatic and entertaining man who never tired of his quest for a great historical discovery. Renowned for his quick wit, which could be disarming, the 9th Duke was once asked by a journalist, curious to know more about his habit of wearing white tie for dinner, whether he ever made do with a dinner jacket in the country. 'Yes,' he quipped in reply, 'when I dine alone with my wife in her bedroom.'

His wife was Kathleen Tennant (known as Kakoo). Uncle Roger told me that his mother was 'very good at looking after all the children and quietly keeping the party going as a hostess. She did a great deal of charity work; as chairman of the Blind Association in Leicester she raised a lot of money; and she used her charms to get money for good causes out of Charlie Chaplin who became a personal friend.'

The 9th Duke's education at Eton and Trinity College, Cambridge, had led to a life-long fascination with archaeology and medieval history. Uncle Roger said that he was 'fantastically clever: he could read Ancient French, understand Roman Shorthand and Early English.' One of Uncle Roger's earliest memories was, he said, of 'scrubbing all the ancient tiles that he had dug up in Byland Abbey in North Yorkshire'. The 13th-century mosaic tiles, and many others the Duke had collected, were eventually given to the British Museum in 1947 in lieu of death duties; they can still be seen there today. His collection and that of Captain Ludovic Lindsay together made up one of the greatest medieval tile collections of the 20th century. It included a number of whole pavements: from Halesowen Abbey, in Worcestershire (now the West Midlands), Burton Lazars, in Leicestershire, and Canynge's House, in Bristol, as well as those from the Cistercian abbey at Byland and from Rievaulx.[42]

Digging up graves, old priories and burial sites was not an uncommon

pastime at that time. The Duke knew all the leading geologists and archaeologists of his day and travelled to Egypt several times in the 1920s to study Tutankhamun's tomb. Kakoo accompanied him on one of his visits and in his diary he describes how Lord Carnarvon, a great admirer of the Duchess, allowed her into the tombs first. All she said when she came out was, to her husband's horrified disgust, 'They were very shiny.'

Various areas around Belvoir were excavated under the Duke's supervision including the 8th Earl of Rutland's crypt in Bottesford Church, in the hope that it might contain some written material by Shakespeare; the site of Belvoir Priory, behind the Dower House, was dug up to look for King John's heart; and extensive trenches were searched on the site of Croxton Abbey, in nearby Croxton Kerrial. Nothing of any consequence was discovered but his enthusiasm never faltered.

OPPOSITE ABOVE *John Manners, the 9th Duke of Rutland,*
1936, by Sir Oswald Birley.
OPPOSITE BELOW A few of the medieval tiles that were
collected by the 9th Duke remain at Belvoir.
RIGHT *Kathleen, 9th Duchess of Rutland, with her Dog Johnny*
Bull, 1933, by Dame Laura Knight. Kathleen (née Tennant),
my husband's grandmother, was always known as Kakoo.
TOP Kakoo with her daughters Ursula and Isobel.
ABOVE Kakoo with Isobel.

RIGHT The 9th Duke was passionate about the family's history and he established the Muniment Room in the 1930s, labelling and cataloguing as much archive material as he could. He was also a collector and regularly bought lots from auctions that interested him or had connections with Belvoir. Many loose estate documents as well as books and ledgers are held in the Muniment Room. BELOW My father-in-law, the Marquis of Granby, as he was then, with his two brothers, Lord John Manners and Lord Roger Manners.

The great physicist Sir Oliver Lodge (best known for his part in the development of wireless communication) also studied the paranormal. Uncle Roger remembers an occasion when Sir Oliver was expected at the castle, and how they all waited for his arrival in the excited hope that he might identify any ghostly presences. 'Sadly,' said Roger, 'it turned out to be very disappointing. This blowsy medium that arrived with him was very ordinary looking, not at all what we were expecting, and no ghosts were sensed at all.'

Less creepy hobbies included shooting, fishing (he was considered to be a very fine game shot and fisherman), ornithology and jewellery design. He had one of the finest collections of British birds' eggs in the country; it is still displayed in our Collections Room. The children used to blow the eggs for him and his diaries are full of bird-watching observations. As for his jewellery design, Carrington's, the London jewellers, were keen to employ him as designer at one time.

What he is best remembered for, however, is his life-long dedication to the restoration of the family's derelict house, Haddon Hall in Derbyshire. 'He understood about houses and was red-hot on medieval history and furniture,' said Roger. He needed to be: Haddon, a fortified medieval manor dating from the 12th century, had been unoccupied for over two centuries and all the roofs had fallen in. 'All the existing

lead was melted down because after 200 years it crystallises and water can get through it: they found 14 per cent of the substance was silver and they made rather a good silver bar out of it.' Can you imagine how exciting it must have been for young children to find silver in an old roof? Kakoo was also very helpful and organized all the beautiful and much-acclaimed replanting schemes in the gardens. It took three years of intensive work, but once the house was habitable the family spent considerable time there as well as at Belvoir.

The 9th Duke's other great achievement was in setting up the family's Muniment Room at Belvoir. While he was

assessing the Old Stables for repairs one day, he came across three unopened boxes on the top floor. When he found the first document, a letter from Lord Nelson, he knew he was looking at a treasure trove. An invoice for cleaning a portrait of William Shakespeare was discovered, which confirmed the 5th Earl's connection with the Bard (see page 25), and then a letter from Charles I offering to pay the Earl of Rutland £1m for various services. Uncle Roger remembers how his father 'took it rather smartly to the Bank of England where he was told, rather more smartly, "Go home!"' When the Second World War broke out he secured the temporary lodging of the National Archives at Belvoir, and the Army Records Office at Haddon. These wise actions contributed to the preservation of the buildings as well as the documents, because they prevented the house and the castle from being requisitioned, as were so many other large country houses.

The Duke died aged only 54 on 21 April 1940, in his Muniment Room, where he had spent so much time cataloguing the archive material: he had been suffering from pneumonia.

THE 10TH DUKE OF RUTLAND, CHARLES JOHN ROBERT MANNERS 1940–99

CHARLES WAS ONLY 20 when he succeeded to the dukedom; at the time he was serving as a subaltern in the Grenadier Guards during the Second World War. He stayed on in the army, rose to the rank of Major and then, having been wounded in France, was sent home in 1945. My father-in-law was a wonderful and charming man who could put anyone at ease. In his youth he was described by Barbara Cartland as 'the handsomest man in England'. He married his first wife, Anne Cumming-Bell, mother of my sister-in-law Charlotte, in 1946 and his second wife, my mother-in-law, Frances Sweeny, in 1958.

Like his father he devoted himself to the continuing restoration of Belvoir and the now-glorious Haddon Hall. Lord John, Charles's younger brother, and his family also spent a lot of time at Haddon making improvements. When Uncle John died, my brother-in-law Edward moved

BELOW An estate party to celebrate the 10th Duke's return from the Second World War.
BOTTOM The 10th Duke in the private Drawing Room when it was panelled, in the mid-1950s.

RIGHT The 10th Duke and his first wife
Anne Cumming-Bell at Belvoir Lodge in
the early 1950s. The dog was one of a
succession of yellow Labradors, all named
either Quest or Belvoir.

BELOW *Frances Sweeny, Duchess of Rutland*,
1963, by Norman Hepple. My mother-in-
law Frances, now the Dowager Duchess,
sat for Norman Hepple at the same time
as her husband.

OPPOSITE *Charles, the 10th Duke of Rutland*
with his Son David with a Yellow Labrador
called Belvoir, 1963, by Norman Hepple.

into a house close to Haddon Hall and took over the
running of the Derbyshire estate with his wife Saskia.

Many local people will remember Charles for his
determination to stop the excavation of coal mines on parts
of the estate and other areas in the beautiful Vale of Belvoir.
In 1976 the National Coal Board had proposed to extract
500 million tons of coal that was estimated to lie beneath
this area of outstanding natural beauty. As the local and
respected County Councillor, Charles whipped up huge
support in opposing this and received thousands of local
signatures for a petition to try to persuade the government
to reconsider its position. He famously announced, 'I shall
put up a great fight. I shall lie down in front of the
bulldozers.' T-shirts were printed with the slogan 'I'll lie
down with the Duke', and many of his supporters,
particularly pretty girls, wore these for a press
demonstration. His campaign was largely successful: by
1982 the proposal had been reduced to one pit outside
Melton Mowbray at Asfordby and the Vale of Belvoir
continued to prosper as the rural community that it had
been for hundreds of years.

Charles died on 1 January 1999, and my husband, David,
became the 11th Duke.

MY TOUR

T IS A CENTURIES-OLD CUSTOM for people to be shown round houses of significance – think of Jane Austen's description in *Pride and Prejudice* of Elizabeth Bennett and her aunt and uncle touring Mr Darcy's house, Pemberley, while he was away. (Opening a house to the paying public for commercial reasons is brand new by comparison, and really only took off with the advent of the National Trust in the late 19th century.) Belvoir was no exception and long before Elizabeth, the 5th Duchess, had finished the building work, word of the splendours of her new castle had spread across the region and sightseers began to arrive in ever increasing numbers.

If visitors were enthralled by what they saw at Belvoir, they must also have been astonished by their guide. Practice at the time allowed a senior member of household staff to conduct tours round a house for a 'consideration'. Anne Keeling, the housekeeper, was assigned to the task at Belvoir. The choice was strange: in fact why she was kept on the staff at all is puzzling. She was a drunk, and her 'dawdling appearance' and inability 'to negotiate the stairs and passages' were a major cause for comment. But whether out of genuine interest in the castle or for tales of the tour's guide, tourists kept coming and by 1821 accounts record that a John Jenkinson was paid 'for attending nineteen Sundays at the Castle, to prevent the intrusion of Strangers'.

Today we have 21 professional guides and 9 volunteers who work here between March and September when the house is open, and who also come in for private groups throughout the year. I take tours too, by special arrangement. I find that they are hardly ever the same twice because more is constantly being discovered about the treasures in the house and the people who lived here. Far from being a moribund relic of the past, the house seems to come more alive with each discovery.

Various leading specialists, in architecture, furniture, paintings and so on, have contributed enormously to our knowledge and comprehension of the collections, and I shall introduce them to you as we go. But perhaps most useful to me in understanding the house are the words of the Revd Irwin Eller and the 8th Duchess. The Revd Eller was the 5th Duke's chaplain;[1] he wrote a thorough description of the castle and its contents in 1841 which gives us an accurate insight into life at Belvoir in the first part of the 19th century. The 8th Duke's wife, Violet, was the only person to make a noticeable impact on the interiors (and gardens) after Elizabeth. She was an accomplished and respected artist, but also pragmatic and, in her typically no-nonsense manner, she filled a notebook with details of alterations she made and the reasons behind them. Both these documents allow us to make fascinating

PREVIOUS PAGES This photograph was inspired by George Sanders' painting of Elizabeth, the 5th Duchess (see page 51); almost nothing in the surrounding landscape has changed in the two centuries between the two pictures.
LEFT An aerial view of the south-west elevation shows the castle and grounds in all their glory.

LEFT One of the many peacocks that thrive in our grounds. They may have been introduced to Belvoir as early as the 12th century, and have been part of the family's Ros coat of arms since the 15th century.
OVERLEAF The south-west front of the castle features the Round Tower, or Regent's Tower as it was renamed by the Prince Regent on his visit here in 1813. The Chapel is to the right with large Gothic windows flanked with turrets. This side of the castle was thankfully spared from the ravaging effects of the fire in 1816 and has remained true to James Wyatt's original magnificent design.

comparisons with the castle as it is today, and the information they contain has given me the courage to make changes of my own. Their words are printed in *italic* in the chapters that follow, to make it easy to distinguish them.

Normally, for the sake of convenience and privacy, tours are restricted to the public rooms. This written tour of the house would not be complete, however, without including some of the personal living space that makes the house our home. Gems such as the medieval remains of the second castle that are now our wine store, a fine group of family portraits by Lely and the Roman-style friezes on the walls of what was Elizabeth's bedroom, would also be missed. So I have gone beyond the visitors' ropes and briefly described our family rooms which are of historic interest.

Before my tour of the inside of the house starts, you may want to look at the exterior. John Martin Robinson made me see it with new eyes when he said, 'The most important thing about Belvoir is the romantic picturesque skyline which is thrilling as you drive towards it; you see the castle on the hill with the towers and turrets and the flag flying.'

The gardens on the terraces below the castle were originally the creation of the 5th Duke's wife, Elizabeth, in the early 19th century. Walkways were carved through 8 acres of new woodlands, lawns were laid and flowerbeds planted. Influenced by ideas garnered from her Grand Tour of Italy, she placed the 15th-century statues by Caius Cibber, which had lined the driveway, among the terraces to give the effect of a Roman hillside. Planting continued through the generations including the creation of the Spring Gardens during the 7th Duke's tenure to provide colour through the hunting season, but it was Violet, wife of the 8th Duke, who was largely responsible for the gardens that we see today. With help from Harold Peto, a notable Edwardian garden designer who was influenced by Italian gardens and by the Arts and Crafts movement, she created a formal scheme, moving the Cibber statues to form part of the permanent framework, with abundant planting to offset the clipped evergreens, paving, balustrades and statuary. As well as on-going maintenance in the gardens, efforts are being made every year to restore the original walkways through the grounds.

The Rose Garden featuring Edwardian fountain and statuary, with one of the Cibber statues on the terrace above.

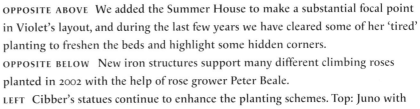

OPPOSITE ABOVE We added the Summer House to make a substantial focal point in Violet's layout, and during the last few years we have cleared some of her 'tired' planting to freshen the beds and highlight some hidden corners.

OPPOSITE BELOW New iron structures support many different climbing roses planted in 2002 with the help of rose grower Peter Beale.

LEFT Cibber's statues continue to enhance the planting schemes. Top: Juno with her insignia, a peacock. Bottom: One of the senses, Taste.

BELOW The Corinthian column in the Rose Garden was acquired from Bologna in Italy for Violet.

Ground plans of the Public Rooms

A Courtyard
1 The Portico
2 The Pre-Guard Room
3 The Guard Room
4 The Old Kitchens and Pastry Room
5 Upper part of the Guard Room
6 The Carriage Landing
7 The 40-Acre Landing

8 The Chapel
9 The Ballroom Stairs
10 The Ballroom
11 The Chinese Dressing Room
12 The Chinese Bedroom
13 The Elizabeth Saloon
14 The State Dining Room
15 The Picture Gallery

16 The King's Sitting Room
17 The King's Bedroom
18 The King's Dressing Room
19 The Earl's Landing
20 The Regent's Gallery
21 The Libraries
22 Upper part of the Chapel

GROUND FLOOR

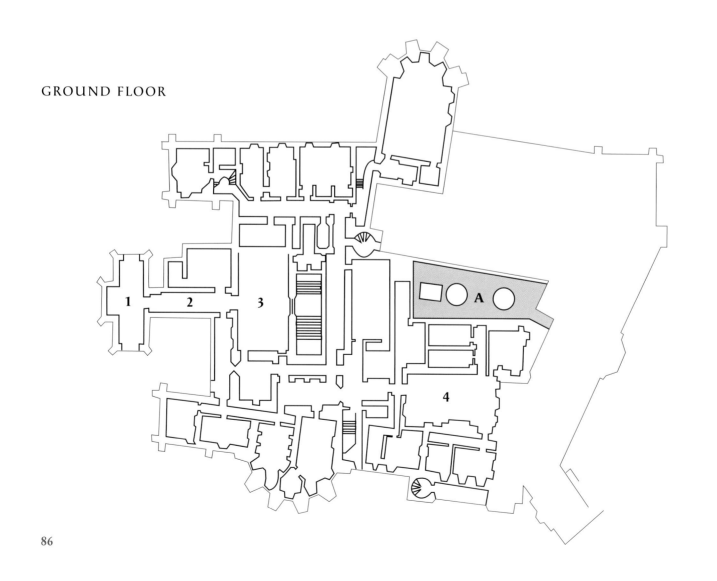

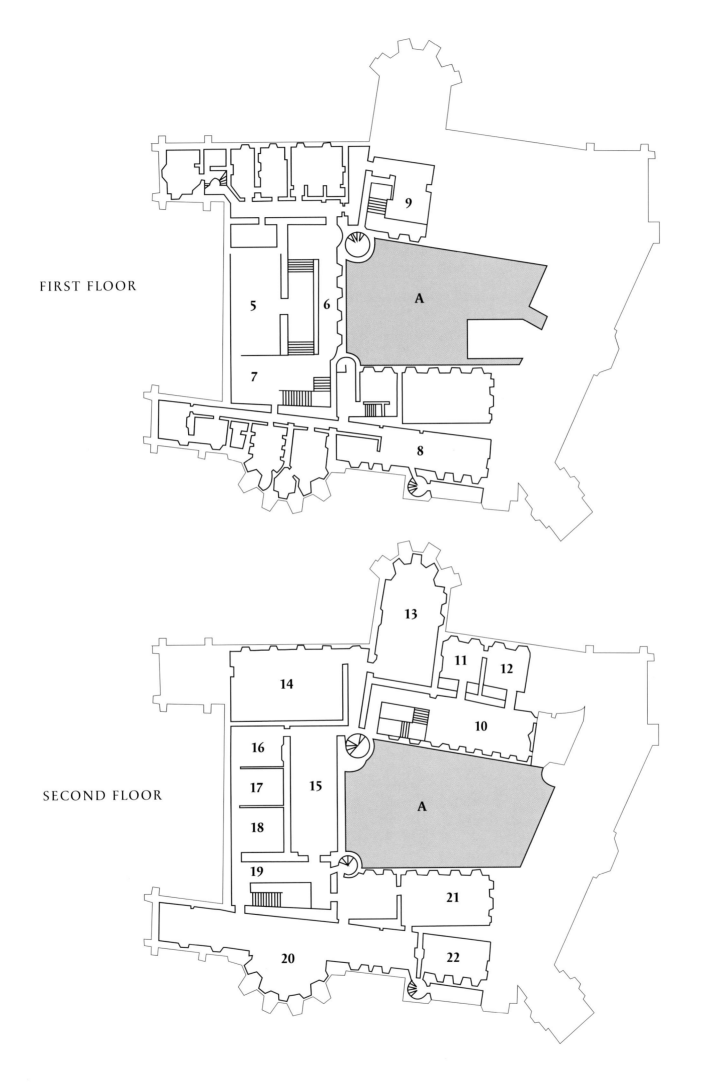

FIRST FLOOR

SECOND FLOOR

The Public Rooms

THE PORTICO

MY TOUR starts from Thoroton's Gothic-style entrance on the north-west side at the vast front doors. These were built to allow carriages through to the Portico, or porte cochère, so that passengers could be dropped off under cover. Before the fire of 1816 destroyed so much of this part of the building, entry was up a small flight of steps straight into the hallway. (Another entrance into the Courtyard on the south-west side was dismantled in 1801 as part of Wyatt's improvements.) Instead of simply rebuilding the steps, Thoroton and Elizabeth extended the entrance from the hall into a long corridor with this drive-through facility at the front.

Parked proudly next to the siege cannon and curricle guns is a 1908 Renault motor car. It was bought after the 8th Duke and his family moved into the castle and was used for excursions across the countryside. His daughter Lady Diana Cooper recalled these drives: 'We were goggled, dust-coated and hatted with peaked motor caps, attached with a six-inch safety pin. There was a fearful smell and dense clouds of dust, causing the horses to shy and adventurers to be jeered and scoffed at.'[2] David still takes it out regularly and in September 2008, to celebrate its centenary, he drove it to Dieppe to join the Dieppe Retro Vintage Car Rally. Both he and the car survived.

LEFT When Sir John Thoroton designed the huge doors into the Portico, he may well have been inspired by similar ones at Haddon Hall. The coat of arms represents the 5th Duke of Rutland and his wife Elizabeth Howard.
RIGHT The Portico is now home to an 18th-century canon and, usually, a vintage Renault car, which was out being 'given a run' when the photograph was taken.

THE PRE-GUARD ROOM

Looking down the long corridor from the finial above the Portico doorway is an enormous elk's head, nicknamed 'Pete' by the staff, which was found in an Irish peat bog and presented to the 4th Duke when he was Lord Lieutenant of Ireland. The Giant Irish Elk has been extinct for a thousand years, so 'Pete' could be very old indeed.

Thoroton's Pre-Guard Room, with its huge ceiling, provides a fine and fitting backdrop to oiled firearms of the historic Leicestershire militia that for many years was controlled by the Lord Lieutenant of the county – a position that every leading member of the Manners family has held from 1667 until 1925. Sufficient 19th-century 'Brown Bess' muskets for 120 men line up next to earlier ones brought over from Dublin by the 4th Duke in the 1780s. Many still have a flint in their firing mechanism, and their powder bags and bayonet scabbards hang alongside them.

The leather water buckets, lined with pitch and decorated with the coronet and cipher, are positioned above the stands of arms and were to use with the fire engine by the front door in case of fire. They are a constant reminder of the devastation of the fire in 1816.

OPPOSITE The Pre-Guard Room is lined with 'Brown Bess' muskets and leather buckets, now filled with sand, which were for use in case of fire, and trophies of a bygone era of game hunting. Above the doorway you can just see the huge antlers of 'Pete', the Giant Elk.
BELOW Looking down the Pre-Guard Room into the Guard Room.

THE GUARD ROOM AND LANDINGS

ELLER WROTE: '*The Guard Room is a magnificent combination of ancient style with modern comfort.*' I'm not sure you could describe it today as 'modern comfort', but all large gatherings, from charity events to our children's parties, begin here. In winter, log fires at either end of the room roar all day. The fireplace on the internal wall raises a lot of interest because it appears to have no chimney. Above it are three arches with views up to the 40-Acre Landing (named for reasons that no one can remember) and the cantilevered Earl's Staircase (an exact copy of the one burnt to dust in the fire). Elizabeth, not one to compromise, had the chimney routed under the floor to avoid spoiling the vista.

This grand hallway, with its huge vaulted ceiling, is another of Thoroton's designs and his love of Gothic-style architecture is presented to maximum effect. Lincoln Cathedral inspired many of his ideas but the stained glass that he put in the windows was replaced with plain glass in the early 1900s by David's grandmother, the 9th Duchess, probably to let in more light and to look less cathedral-like.

The tops of the two huge tables in here are said by Eller to be made from strips of old wooden pipes from one of the family's mines in Derbyshire. The frames and legs are oak and were allegedly found '*under some old houses in Sheffield*'. The provenance is curious but the tables are particularly handsome and we use them almost daily.

For the military enthusiast this room is another showcase for weapons and armour. The walls are covered with more flintlock muskets from the Leicestershire Militia and circles of swords, dating from 1760, bearing the Duke of Wellington's head cast on a centre medallion. Wellington was a great friend of the 5th Duke and a regular visitor to Belvoir; a whole suite of rooms was dedicated to his use.

Other displays include a series of short swords or 'hangers' dating from 1751, with 'Leicester M' engraved on their hilts, arranged in small circles, with larger circles of long straight-bladed swords. These were used by the 21st (Granby's) Light Dragoons, a regiment that was raised and equipped by the legendary Marquis of Granby whom military expert Stephen Wood believes to have been one of the greatest British soldiers of the 18th century. Two of Granby's basket-hilted broadswords are in here: the one he used when he served on the Duke of Cumberland's staff during the Jacobite rebellion of 1745–6 and one he probably carried as Colonel of the Royal Regiment of Horse Guards. A portrait of him by Sir Joshua Reynolds, in the State Dining Room, shows him in uniform carrying this particular sword. One of his early sporting guns, mounted in silver with 1763 London hallmarks, also hangs here.

Encased behind glass in the wall by the staircase is a grenadier's embroidered cloth 'mitre cap', of the Duke of Rutland's Regiment of Foot (1745–6). In 1745 just 15 English noblemen raised regiments for the defence of their country against the

OPPOSITE The Guard Room never fails to impress visitors, partly for its superb ceiling and display of armour, but also for the views through the arches. The chimney of the fireplace was cleverly angled to run backwards below the floor of the 40-Acre Landing behind it, in order to allow views of the cantilevered staircase beyond. It has always confused people; my father-in-law liked to add to their confusion by saying, 'Oh, the smoke goes up the chimney just the same.'
BELOW The basket-hilted 16th-century broadsword belonged to the family's military hero, the Marquis of Granby, who was revered for his part in the Seven Years War. It is leaning against one of the massive oak tables described by Eller.

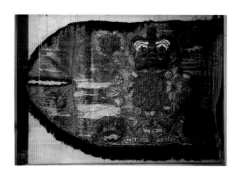 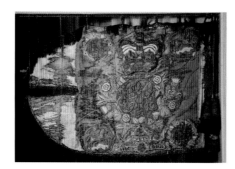 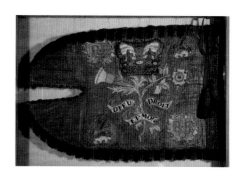

Jacobite rebellion, and the 3rd Duke of Rutland was one of them. The cap is the only item of uniform known to have survived from the Duke's short-lived regiment and is a very rare example of a British soldier's mitre cap to have survived.

The colours of the Leicestershire Militia and the Garter banners of the Dukes of Rutland hang over the stairs above the arch. Either side, in two other arches, are the ornamental leather and wood figures of soldiers fashioned by James Wyatt's son, the painter and sculptor Matthew Cotes Wyatt.

Tim Knox, director of Sir John Soane's Museum and former head curator of the National Trust, described this series of three rooms to me as 'one of the most theatrical and successful entrances in any country house or castle – it puts Windsor Castle in the shade'. He went on to say, 'The elegant Gothic tracery of grey stone, combining Norman motifs with Perpendicular vaulting, and its astonishing displays of serried weaponry, leaves the visitor in no doubt as to the status and antiquity of its ducal proprietor.'

Leaving the Guard Room and mounting the stairs to the Carriage Landing, named after the 7th Duke's invalid carriage which has been left here, you pass under George Sanders' full-size portraits of the 5th Duke in his coronation robes on one side and his Duchess, with a crayon in her hand, on the other. When Eller wrote his book these pictures were in the Elizabeth Saloon, 'fixed in frames with pedestals'. Eller informs us that originally 'frames of the most costly description' were made for them but it was decided not to hang them in the conventional way and the frames were stored. Violet's diary refers

to them in a peculiar manner: 'King Edward VII's ever recurring questions to me used to be "Have you got rid of them yet?!!!"' We can only assume that she had them framed as they were originally intended and hung them where they are now.

Three embroidered silk guidons of the Marquis of Granby's 21st Light Dragoons³ are displayed in glass frames at the top of the staircase. Stephen Wood tells me that they are an immensely interesting group of flags, perhaps the most important group of such items to survive in private hands in Britain. They are a reminder of the short life of a little-known light cavalry regiment, raised by the Marquis of Granby, in the midst of the Seven Years War (1756–63) and disbanded soon after. Thanks to their careful preservation over the years, they are among the earliest British examples of their kind and certainly the only group of three regimental guidons of that period known to survive.

Further towards the 40-Acre Landing, at the bottom of the Earl's Staircase, hang a trio of portraits of the Marquis of Granby's German allies during the Seven Years War.

ABOVE Three guidons of the Marquis of Granby's 21st Light Dragoons. The regiment commandeered horses from the Belvoir Hunt in 1760 to support the cavalry.

LEFT The mitre cap, said to belong to Captain T. Welsh, from the Duke of Rutland's Regiment of Foot (1745–6).

RIGHT Above a fireplace in the Guard Room are portraits of three monarchs who have stayed at the castle: *James I*, after Daniel Mytens; *Charles I*, by a follower of Sir Anthony van Dyck; and *Queen Mary II*, circle of William Wissing. The books come from the castle archives.

On the Carriage Landing is the invalid carriage used by the 7th Duke in his later years. His granddaughter Lady Diana Cooper remembered him being wheeled around in it. Other items include a penny-farthing bicycle and a sleigh that was a present to Lady Diana's eldest sister, Marjorie, from an ardent admirer, Prince Felix Youssupoff.

LEFT The Guard Room stairs lead on one side to the Carriage Landing, and to the 40-Acre Landing on the other. The 8th Duke of Rutland's Garter flag from St George's Chapel, Windsor, hangs over an Indian cannon captured during the first Sikh War and presented to the 5th Duke by Henry, 1st Viscount Hardinge, Governor General of India, in 1848. The suits of armour are made up from pieces which mostly date from the 14th- and 15th-centuries, though from the knee down they are Victorian.

ABOVE From the left: *Prince Ferdinand, Duke of Brunswick-Luneburg; Frederick, Count of Schaumburg-Lippe-Buckeburg; Charles, Hereditary Prince of Brunswick-Luneburg, all 1759, by Johann George Ziesenis.* The portraits were commissioned by the Marquis of Granby in tribute to the loyalty and friendship of his German colleagues.

RIGHT The penny farthing is believed to have belonged to the Rector of Bottesford Church, the Revd F. J. Norman. He was the 5th Duke's nephew and was married to his first cousin, Lady Adeliza Manners. One can only hope he didn't use it to try and cycle up the tortuously steep hill to the castle.

THE BALLROOM

ELLER DESCRIBED this as the 'Grand Corridor'; apparently it was used as a ballroom only occasionally. Essentially it is a large, grand link from the Picture Gallery and State Dining Room to the Ballroom Stairs and Tapestry Room, taking in the Chinese Rooms along the way. Thoroton was responsible for the design and, influenced as he was by Lincoln Cathedral and the Gothic style, he created this huge space, 120 feet long and 24 feet wide, with nine windows of etched glass to block the view into the courtyard. The windows are edged in stained glass, which was considered ugly in the 1930s, so David's grandmother Kakoo painted them white; they are due to be restored. Thoroton died before the room was complete but his brother, the Revd Charles Roos Thoroton, was able to finish it.

BELOW The Ballroom was the perfect size for popular dances during the Regency period. It is now licensed for weddings to be held here, and is also sometimes used for wedding breakfasts.

RIGHT Above the central pier at each end end of the Ballroom are the arms of the 5th Duke as Knight of the Garter and those of the Howard family for his wife. Here they are in stained glass; at the other end they are echoed in painted relief.

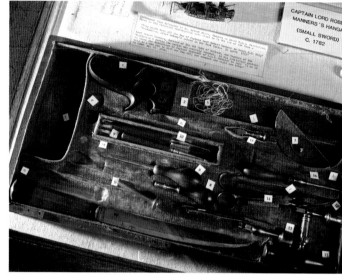

The walls are lined with family portraits: a posthumous picture of Lord Granby's second son, Captain Lord Robert Manners, by Sir Joshua Reynolds is a particular favourite of mine, although Michael Hall, of Hazlitt, Gooden & Fox, an expert in portraits and Old Masters, believes that Reynolds seems to have lacked the vital inspiration which he acquired from living sitters. The subject, Lord Robert, a celebrated naval officer, died from wounds sustained in action on board his ship, HMS *Resolution*, at the Battle of the Saintes during the American War of Independence on 12 April 1782. His arm was broken and he was wounded in both legs, so severely in one that it needed to be amputated. After the operation he was sent back to England but

ABOVE LEFT *The Death of Lord Robert Manners*, by Thomas Stothard. (This usually hangs in the private rooms.)
ABOVE RIGHT These gruesome instruments are said to have been used by the ship's surgeon, Dr Robert Blair, to amputate Lord Robert Manners' leg when he was on board HMS Resolution.
LEFT *Captain Lord Robert Manners 1758–1782, Son of 1st Marquis of Granby,* by Sir Joshua Reynolds.
OPPOSITE LEFT The Ballroom Stairs that lead from the Carriage Landing were rebuilt by Sir John Thoroton after the 1816 fire. The shaped screen, disguised with a tapestry, shields our rather unruly private rooms from public view.
OPPOSITE RIGHT Immediately above the stairs are portraits of the 1st Duke of Rutland with his third wife, Lady Catherine Noel.

developed tetanus on the way and died at sea. The knife allegedly used to remove the limb, however, arrived safely at Belvoir and it is displayed in a cabinet opposite the Reynolds portrait.

Violet wrote: '*We have sung a lot in the ballroom and Marjorie* [her eldest daughter] *and her voice will always be remembered by its walls.*' She describes dances in here when she was first married and children dancing with morris men in '*every lively style*' in 1884 but, judging by the amount of furniture that she lists as being here, there wouldn't have been much space left for dancing. In the early 1900s the walls were painted to resemble blocks of stone with diamond-patterned stonework around the windows, and the windows were hung with stone-coloured curtains that pooled on the window seats. Nine sofas in blues and yellows with several single chairs and footstools to match, and a piano, completed the look. I don't know what happened to the curtains but I have never seen any in here.

Other than a coat of paint very little has changed in this room. It is often used for talks or corporate presentations and for these events requires very little furniture except rows of temporary chairs (and on these occasions can seat up to 70). There have been many parties here in my memory but, even without so much furniture, I don't think it really works for large numbers.

THE CHINESE ROOMS

LEADING OFF THE BALLROOM is a suite of rooms named for the walls that are decorated in the Chinese manner of the 19th century. There is a bedroom, a dressing room and what was a sitting room which is now called the Wellington Room (the last is now part of our private wing). Tim Knox tells me that 'The 5th Duke's sequence of Chinoiserie rooms, all slightly different, epitomize the very best and most expensive Regency taste', and that they are for him 'one of the great surprises at Belvoir Castle'. The surprise to me is that the wallpaper in two of the rooms is probably older than the date of Elizabeth's rebuilding, according to John Martin Robinson. We don't have any documentation about it: another mystery.

The walls of the Bedroom are covered in exquisite silk panels painted with Chinese figures and landscapes. Violet's youngest daughter, Lady Diana Cooper, traced them and recreated the design in her London house.

We think the now half-tester bed was once a full tester. It is topped with a domed George I canopy but the material is worn in several places. My mother-in-law found a pair of silk curtains in the same damask when we were sorting through a laundry room so we are fortunate that we have a match, but it raised the question as to whether there had been posts at the bottom of the bed too. Before we rip into the material to mend the canopy, it would be nice to try and find the other posts.

According to some guests, the Chinese Room is haunted. American friends seem to be a particular target and many have spluttered that they have felt a slap on the head if they have not removed a cap!

LEFT The bed in the Chinese Bedroom is early Victorian, but its elaborate domed canopy dates from the reign of George I (and so is likely to have been in the previous castle). I added an Indian sari as a bedcover. The panels of Chinese silk that cover the walls also pre-date the room, but we don't know where they came from.
RIGHT ABOVE A detail of one of the panels shows how beautifully they were painted.
RIGHT BELOW I assume that Violet brought the Dresden clock into this room to complement the Dresden chandelier that she hung in the Dressing Room next door.

An internal door takes you into the Dressing Room. The wallpaper is sadly damaged and there is a distinctive strip, about 15 inches wide, running round the top in a faded grey colour with the foliage pattern painted in white. It has been suggested that the paper may have come from a smaller room, possibly even from the previous castle. The family's story is that the 5th Duchess discovered it rolled up in a cupboard and kept it to use later, but when the building was finished, the panels were found to be too short and someone had to paint in the top.

Violet brought the Dresden chandelier from the private Drawing Room; like the Dresden clock in the Bedroom, it may have come from Cheveley or even the previous castle. The Dresden porcelain clock on the mantelpiece in here, however, is a later addition; it is mid-19th century and signed Inglis.

Pictures have been hung in here over the years but personally I think they rather spoil the paper. However, *The Ox-Stall* painted by David Teniers the Younger towards the end of his career is beautiful and a faithful depiction of a magnificent bull being presented by its proud owner.

THE ELIZABETH SALOON

OF ALL THE ROOMS, no other captures the essence of the castle's creator or the Regency period more than the Elizabeth Saloon. The Duchess and her husband visited Paris (after Napoleon had been imprisoned on Elba) in 1814 and she returned bursting with ideas for a 'Louis Quatorze'-style drawing room. So successful was the end result – the first French interior of its kind in England – that it was copied all over Mayfair and in grand country houses throughout the 19th century. Tragically, she was never to see it in its full glory. She had shielded its development from family and friends to intensify its grand opening on her husband's birthday, but there were no celebrations. As the room entered its final stages of completion, she died suddenly from appendicitis. This jewel in her crown, which epitomized her style and hedonism, was renamed the Elizabeth Saloon in her memory.

Its splendour was finally unveiled at a party for her husband's birthday four years later in 1829. The Duke of Wellington's mistress, Harriet Arbuthnot, a guest, wrote: 'It is the most magnificent room I ever saw, fitted up in the style of Louis 14th in panels of blue silk damask and the most beautiful carving and gilding.'[4]

A marble sculpture of Elizabeth is placed so that she appears to be walking into the room through an ornate floor-to-ceiling looking glass. The sculptor, Matthew Cotes Wyatt, the youngest son of James Wyatt, is also credited with the design and the decoration of the room, the painted ceiling, and with purchasing the *boiserie* (panelling) and the furniture. The *boiserie* was always thought to have originally

LEFT The Louis XIV-style Saloon was devised by Elizabeth as a backdrop for entertaining on a befittingly grand scale, the quantity of gilt and ormolu furniture all adding to the spectacle. It is easy to imagine friends and family over the years having drinks here before dinner and returning later to play cards on one of the many embossed-velvet-topped tables.
RIGHT The statue of Elizabeth was sculpted by Matthew Cotes Wyatt, in 1826, a year after her death. Her friend Mrs Arbuthnot wrote that it was 'excessively like her'.
OVERLEAF The opulent Elizabeth Saloon is the only room in the castle to have remained essentially unchanged since it was finished.

belonged to Madame de Maintenon (the morganatic second wife of Louis XIV) but textile historian Annabel Westman explained to me that it is dated several years after her death and more likely to have come from a Parisian hôtel of about 1735.

There were originally two sets of gilt seat furniture in here, one covered with Beauvais tapestry and the other with a rich Chinese silk, 'partly coloured with crimson ground'.[5] Eller describes the fabric as '*blue satin damask embroidered with crimson flowers*'. The chairs were re-upholstered by my mother-in-law in pale blue and crimson patterned damask. The seat furniture, together with gilt console tables, five marble-topped commodes with ormolu mounts, 'a quantity of beautiful ornaments of ormolu' and a 'large marqueterie Commode secretaire' were offered to the Duke by Matthew Cotes Wyatt at the same time as the *boiserie* for the grand total of 1,450 guineas.[6]

The carpet, specially woven for the room, with peacock motifs at the corners to match the painted peacocks on the ceiling and a large oval medallion in the centre, was also supplied in 1824 and cost £165.[7] For many years it was mistakenly believed to be a Savonnerie (knotted pile) or an

Aubusson (tapestry weave) carpet, but Annabel assures me that it is in fact a Wilton or cut-loop pile carpet (moquette frisé) woven in 27-inch wide strips and sewn together. It was supplied by a M. Le Fevre,[8] probably Leopold-Henri-Joseph Lefebvre, Director of Piat Lefebvre et Fils, the most important carpet manufactory in Tournai, Belgium, from 1801 to 1844.[9]

Elizabeth seems to have lost sight of how much everything was costing and if there had been a budget, it would have been far exceeded. Indeed some of her letters during this time expressed surprise at the expense of some items. But purchases continued. Her friend Colonel Trench charged £57 15s. for 'a Cabinet ornamented with rare Slabs of Turquoise and ormoulu mounts' that he had bought from Jarman of 130 New Bond Street.[10]

Perhaps the most extraordinary feature of the room is the ceiling, which is divided into four main compartments – a circular one in the bay and three semi-circular ones. Elizabeth had discussed the designs in detail with Matthew Cotes Wyatt before her death, and the result is the depiction of the myth of Jupiter and Io, in which Jupiter transforms his lover, Io, into a white heifer to conceal her from his wife Juno. There are different interpretations of the scenes, but I see Elizabeth as Io to the Duke of York's Jupiter, although it has also been said that her widower, the Duke of Rutland, preferred to see her as Juno. In addition to the allegorical scenes, in each corner of the ceiling and in the centre are portraits of the 5th Duke and Duchess, Colonel Frederick Trench, and the Duke and Duchess's surviving children: Lord George Manners, Lady Adeliza Manners, Lady Catherine Jermyn, the Marquis of Granby and Lord John Manners. Their deceased children are represented as angels.

Apart from doing some careful restoration and meticulous cleaning, no one has ever changed this room. Before my mother-in-law moved out she very generously

LEFT Top left: *Sacrifice*, French School, *c.*1700, is one of a set of four Classical scenes set into the silk wall panels.
Top right: Inset with *pietra dura* decorative details, the two French mid-17th-century ebony and giltwood side cabinets were almost certainly supplied by Robert Hume, *c.*1825.
Bottom left: Elizabeth hand painted this gilt-wood table cabinet with flowers and foliage. It is the only example of her painting that we have on show, and reveals her to have been a highly accomplished artist.
Bottom right: One of four gilded peacocks that are set into the cornice. My father-in-law once admitted to David that he shot the leg off with an air rifle in 1937. No explanation was given.
ABOVE A portrait of the 5th Duke, painted by Matthew Cotes Wyatt, is part of the ceiling design.

restored the carpet, which was partly in shreds. It was cleaned and repaired on a massive scaffolding loom; it was attached to a new backing for support before all the tears could be couched. It took two years, two months and two days and cost £100,000.

There is a consensus of opinion that this room should never really be used in order to protect the carpet, but we feel strongly that this is a family house, so we do, on occasion, use it for drinks before big dinner parties in the State Dining Room. It was also used as a film set for *Young Victoria* as a double for a drawing room at Windsor Castle; but for this the carpet was removed and replaced with one from the props department.

We have placed a recent group family portrait by Russian artist Vasili Smirnov (see page 217) here until we can find somewhere more suitable to put it.

Aunt Ursie helped me with the layout of the furniture. It is as she remembered it when, aged 17, she glimpsed Winston Churchill on a sofa near the fire with tears in his eyes as he listened to the news of Edward VIII's abdication on the wireless.

LEFT The myth of Jupiter and Io appears on the ceiling of the Elizabeth Saloon, painted by Matthew Cotes Wyatt. When it was finished, Jupiter looked so like the Duke of York, Elizabeth's close friend and probably her lover, that Wyatt was ordered by Royal command to disguise him. Wyatt gave Jupiter a beard in two of the scenes, but somehow neglected the third.
Top: Jupiter, without a beard, is represented with his mythological insignia, the eagle and thunderbolts, dispatching Mercury on a mission to rescue Io from Argus, the hundred-eyed watchman who had been charged with looking after Io by Juno.
Middle: Jupiter, here with a beard, and his wife Juno with her insignia, a peacock, are seen opposite Mercury with his arm around Venus, who is receiving a flying Cupid; behind her are two children, with Io disguised as a white heifer.
Bottom: Jupiter, again with a beard, with Cupid and Venus.
RIGHT The final catastrophe, the consequence of Juno's jealous rage when she discovers that Jupiter has seduced Io, is represented in the circular compartment of the bay. Juno in her chariot, attended by two peacocks, one in his pride, is giving directions to Iris, who is taking the eyes out of the head of Argus, who has been killed by Mercury.

THE STATE DINING ROOM

As you would expect, the State Dining Room is close to the Elizabeth Saloon, which is, in effect, the State Drawing Room. As you leave the French-style Elizabeth Saloon you walk across the Ballroom landing and into the Roman-style State Dining Room. John Martin Robinson explains that the Gothic architecture fwas avoured by John Thoroton, and the various differing styles used by the Wyatts for the interiors were typical of Regency taste. Windsor Castle is another example of the eclecticism of the period but he believes Belvoir exemplifies it better than any other house because every facet is represented here.

The coffered ceiling of the State Dining Room was copied from the Church of Santa Maria Maggiore in Rome after Elizabeth and the Duke visited Italy in the early 1800s. It is made of deep panels and ribs, filled with stucco flowers in high relief. Unlike its Roman counterpart, the carved flowers at Belvoir are all different. Along the walls there are five arched marble recesses, decorated with vines, which flank five sideboards. These, and other items, were supplied by Gillow, who presented a bill that amounted to £5,881 9s. 1¼d. The sum aroused consternation

LEFT The State Dining Room was the scene of many of the 5th Duke's birthday parties each January, when a different display of plate was used every day during the celebrations. The mighty table can be extended to seat 30 in comfort. Here it is ready for a large family dinner in the early summer.

RIGHT *Charles Manners, 4th Duke of Rutland*, by Sir Joshua Reynolds. An earlier Reynolds portrait of Charles, commissioned by the 3rd Duke, was burnt in the fire of 1816 and this version was a present from the Prince Regent to the 5th Duke of Rutland.

OVERLEAF The room comes into its own in the evening when the table glitters with the family's 1660s silver-gilt and the candles are ablaze.

from the Duke, who questioned the furniture-makers. It transpired, however, that Thoroton had taken responsibility for the transaction and so he was subjected to the wrath of the Duke, who accused him of being 'a dead hand at creating expense, but a very bad one at saving'.[11]

The Grecian chimneypieces cost £715 13s. 3d. and were made by Smith's in London. Above each of them is a magnificent full-length portrait: one of the famous Marquis of Granby, and the other of the 4th Duke of Rutland, both painted by Sir Joshua Reynolds. The Prince Regent generously gave the picture of the Marquis to the 5th Duke after the fire in 1816 had destroyed a similar one of his grandfather, also by Reynolds.

But perhaps the most impressive sight in here is the intricately carved marble side table by Matthew Cotes Wyatt, upon which is set a 17th-century silver punch bowl. Having expended so much effort in the Elizabeth Saloon, Wyatt turned his attention to the Dining Room. There he carved the marble table to resemble a napkin, '*the folds of which are so accurately represented in the marble, as to require a close inspection to convince the observer of the solidity of the material*', wrote Eller. Its weight, of between 2 and 3 tons, required extra support to the floor. The punch bowl, made by Church in 1682, is engraved with a large coat of arms, crest and the Earl's coronet. It weighs 1,979 ounces and cost £616 10s.

Eller describes the room next to this as the Hunters' Dining Room; it is now a commercial kitchen that services banquets and functions in the State Dining Room for up to 250 people. We have recreated the Hunters' downstairs for our shoot dinners and smaller dinner parties.

LEFT ABOVE *Lady Marjorie Manners, Lord John Manners and Lord Haddon, c.1894,* by Sir James Jebusa Shannon. (This hangs in the Picture Gallery.) This triple portrait gave me the idea of photographing my three eldest children – when they were tiny – in the silver punch bowl, for a Christmas card.

LEFT BELOW The punch bowl is displayed on what looks like a double layer of tablecloths; in fact these are made of white marble, and form part of the stand by Matthew Cotes Wyatt.

RIGHT One of the five massive sideboards supplied by Gillow to fit in the arched marble recesses. I have dressed the sideboards with modern china and glass to make them look less bare.

THE PICTURE GALLERY

WHEN THE 4TH DUKE DIED aged 33 in 1787 his eldest son, the 5th Duke, was only nine. The pictures were entrusted into the care of the Revd Peters, Rector of Knipton and Associate of the Royal Academy. Eller quotes him as saying: '*John, the third Duke of Rutland, and Charles, the late much lamented owner of these works, were both of them patrons of the arts, in the fullest extent of the word; for they were not contented only to look at and admire the dawning of genius in the infant mind, but sought out excellence where it could be found.*' When Elizabeth and Wyatt began on their project to rebuild the castle, a new picture gallery was an essential part of the plan, and the finished room does more than justice to the collection.

OPPOSITE The lunette windows bring in the necessary daylight, while the sumptuous, gilded Roman-style friezework forms a magnificent frame for the Picture Gallery's treasures.
BELOW The gallery was badly damaged in the 1816 fire and had to be rebuilt. In addition to the many fine works of art displayed in here is the bed made for Katherine, Countess of Rutland, in 1696.

The design of the room, in Roman style, is thought to be an adaption of James Wyatt's sketches which were drawn up by Thomas Cochran under Thoroton's instruction.[12] Large lunette windows similar to those that Wyatt built at Dodington Park, in Gloucestershire, are another indicator of his hand in this design. Eller describes the room without furniture: '*There is nothing to distract the attention of the visitor from the invaluable treasures in the gallery, except six chairs, exquisitely carved, from the Borghese Palace, at Rome.*' They are still here and the crimson-cloth walls he describes have been renewed but are still here too. Violet notes in her book that Janetta, second wife of the 7th Duke, had covered the '*lovely carved arm chairs, but the silk, with the top light, faded at once*'. That is probably why they are covered in cream silk damask today. The marble

columns supporting four candelabras were no doubt moved when electricity was installed but Violet remembers them for a different reason. She wrote: '*On one of the columns there is a small hole near the door to the Ballroom, caused by little ten-year-old Diana playing hide and seek. The piece off her front tooth was never found! But clever dentistry has repaired her tooth at 17!*'

Violet arranged the green velveteen with the fawn-coloured silk fringe that is on the miniature table that belonged to her son John. (She used the same fringe, which she had bought from a shop in Stamford, to trim the curtains in the bedroom of her daughter Marjorie.)

Before anyone has a chance to study the pictures they always ask me about the bed. For much of the 19th century it was at Haddon Hall but it was brought back to Belvoir in the

1920s. Annabel Westman believes it is one of the most magnificent treasures in the house. It was made in 1696 for Katherine, wife of Lord Ros (later 2nd Duke), and given to her by her father-in-law, to celebrate the birth of her first-born, his grandson John. The couple's entwined cipher – JK and R – is on the tester, and on the headboard beneath the Earl's coronet. It is one of the few surviving examples made by the French upholsterer Francis Lapiere, who was working in Britain.[13] It cost £423 3s., and was paid for in two instalments. The crimson and red cut-silk velvet cost £166. 18s. 6d. and was

supplied by London silk mercer William Sherrard; he also supplied fabrics to William III. Unfortunately, no bills survive for the magnificent trimmings and the rich embroidery depicting animals and birds exquisitely worked on white satin on the tester, backcloth, headboard and linings of the curtains. The coverlet is from an earlier bed made in 1692 for the marriage of the 1st Duke's daughter, Lady Katherine Manners, to Lord John Leveson-Gower.[14] We are grateful to the 9th Duke, David's grandfather, for restoring the bed and bringing it back to Belvoir from Haddon Hall. It is one of the few pieces of furniture that date from the earlier Charles II castle.

In a glass case in the middle of the room is the Elizabeth I silver-gilt and agate ewer and basin set, bearing 1579 and 1581 London hallmarks. It is a 'very rare example of an

FAR LEFT *Shepherd and Shepherdess,* by Thomas Gainsborough, was bought by the 4th Duke in 1787. It hangs between the chairs, c.1700–20, which were acquired for the 5th Duke from the Borghese Palace in Rome in 1820.
LEFT The late 17th-century bed is one of the few items of furniture that is known to come from the third castle. It was a gift from the 1st Duke to his daughter-in-law Katherine, to celebrate the birth of her first child, a son, John, later 3rd Duke.
ABOVE The 16th-century agate and gilt ewer and basin set was a christening present to the 3rd Duke and Duchess of Rutland's third child, William, from George II.

aristocratic order which embodies the characteristic qualities of rich ornament and exotic material.'[15]

The paintings fall into two categories: portraits and Old Masters. Interestingly, nearly all the portraits and landscapes were bought to hang at the castle. The family's London houses, with the exception of Rutland House in Knightsbridge, were rented out and already furnished and hung with pictures. I am enormously grateful to Michael Hall for helping me piece together the information that we have on the collection.

The portraits cover a very wide group of subjects, not just members of the Manners family, but also the kings and queens of England who were involved with the family's history, Manners' friends and relations, husbands and wives, children, mothers- and fathers-in-law, their favourite dogs and horses, their several houses and properties, not least Belvoir itself. Almost every school of English artists is represented, including those distinguished foreigners who came to ply their trade in Britain from the late 16th century onwards. The Earls of Rutland in the late 16th and 17th centuries were not great collectors of paintings – few people were in those days, other than of portraits. Despite losing nearly half the pictures in the 1816 fire, we still have a wide-ranging group of images of the early owners of the castle and of the castle itself, including works by Daniel Mytens, Johann-Baptist Closterman, Jan Siberecht, Jan Griffier the Younger and Marcus Gheeraedts.

Sporting art, dating from the golden age of hunting, by Ben Marshall and his one-time apprentice John Ferneley and later by Sir Alfred Munnings is dotted around the castle. But examples of work from many of these artists are exhibited in the Picture Gallery.

Sir John Guinness, a friend and portrait specialist, was looking at the pictures with me not so long ago and, while picking out his favourites, refreshed my knowledge about some of them too. The full-length portrait of Henry VIII after Holbein is almost iconic and never goes unnoticed. It

was bought by Mr Miller for the 4th Duke from the 4th Viscount Torrington's anonymous sale at Christie's on 24 January 1787 for £211.10s. (and appeared in the Royal Academy's 1953 exhibition, *Kings and Queens AD 653–1953*). In the same year the 4th Duke also bought the three pictures by Thomas Gainsborough.

Reynolds recommended William Marlow to go to Dublin to paint pictures for the 4th Duke when the Duke was Lord Lieutenant of Ireland but Marlow declined, saying he had 'quitted business'. Instead, the Duke commissioned the Irish painter Solomon Delane to paint the four Dublin scenes and Vice-Regal Lodge in Phoenix Park; they cost 65 guineas.

English artists of the late 18th century are particularly well represented at Belvoir, largely through the patronage

of the 4th Duke and his relationship with Reynolds who, as President of the Royal Academy for nearly twenty years, had his finger on the pulse of artistic life in Britain. Portraiture in all its forms was an abiding passion for the Manners family, portraits of themselves, their houses and even their animals. One of the greatest animal painters of the age, indeed probably of any age, was George Stubbs and there are three important and comparatively unknown animal paintings by him in here displayed with a Reynolds portrait of the Marquis of Granby (later the 5th Duke) with his sister Lady Elizabeth Manners as children, with the family's dogs, Turk and Crab. Lord Granby, later the 4th Duke, had earlier commissioned Stubbs to make portraits of these dogs, his two favourites: Turk, a large and hairy Dutch Barge Dog or Keeshound, and Crab, a type of mutt. Both pictures are signed and dated: *Turk* in 1777, and *Turk and Crab* the following year. Stubbs charged £40 for *Turk* but possibly more for the double portrait.

Stubbs' earliest work in our collection is a scene of a lion attacking a stag, a variant of his favourite composition of a lion attacking a horse, which itself derives from a Classical sculpture he saw in Rome in 1754. Seventeen versions of the horse and lion theme by Stubbs are recorded, but very few with a stag. Ours (undated) is set amongst rocks and caves that he had seen at Creswell Crags, a picturesque spot not far from Belvoir on the Duke of Portland's estate at Welbeck.

A large seascape by William van de Velde the Younger, signed and dated 1692, shows the flag ship of Admiral Cornelis Evertsen, the *Hollandia*, the two-decker built in 1683 and carrying 74 guns. Admiral Evertsen, a hero of the Dutch wars against England in the late 17th century, was a commander of the fleet of William of Orange, who became William III when he acceded to the throne with his wife, Mary II, in 1688, therefore becoming an ally of the English rather than an enemy. Reynolds advised the 4th Duke and his father, Lord Granby, on buying pictures from the Dutch, Italian and Spanish schools. His advice, which was gratefully received, is the reason for much of Belvoir's fine collection of Old Masters, particularly Dutch 17th-century works. Though the Van de Velde is unlikely to have been bought on Reynolds' recommendation, several other works including *The Prayer Before the Meal* by Jan Steen were certainly bought by him for the Duke. Reynolds bought many pictures by the Flemish-born Teniers the Younger for his own collection and encouraged others to do the same. The 4th Duke, again on Reynolds' guidance, bought *The Proverbs*, regarded by some experts to be one of Teniers' most important works (others have described it as 'curious, rather than pleasing'). It is one of the largest and most important of his works in our collection and depicts 43 Dutch proverbs. He was astonishingly successful in combining all the different figures and occupations into one composition, though the meanings of several are obscure.

Three large works by Thomas Gainsborough also hang in here, two horizontal landscapes which can be regarded as a pair, and an upright showing a rustic view of a man carrying a stack of firewood on his back as he approaches a cottage with figures standing at the door. This is an historically as well as artistically important work of the early 1780s – it was exhibited at the Royal Academy in 1782 – in that it is the first time Gainsborough used the cottage door, the motif that became so popular in his work.

We have several full-length portraits by both Marcus Gheeraedts and William Larkin. Among the finest is Gheeraedts' portrayal of Frances, Countess of Rutland, in a magnificent dress and jewels. Her son-in-law was the Duke of Buckingham, the ill-fated favourite and minister of James I and Charles I. Edward Bower's portrait of Charles I is very sombre and Michael Hall thinks it was almost certainly based on drawings that the painter made in Westminster Hall during his trial, just days before his execution. It is surprising that the Earl of Rutland, a moderate Parliamentarian, had a portrait of him at all.

I love the pictures of the more recent family members: two portraits of Violet by Sir James Jebusa Shannon, and two paintings by Laura Knight: one of Violet's children, and one of David's grandmother Kakoo with the bulldog she named Johnny Bull. Shannon and Knight would have been considered unusual choices of artists at the time but reflect the informal taste of Violet and of her son. Living in a house with so many echoes of those who have lived here before me is strangely comforting. Looking at the portraits of Violet and Elizabeth and of all the other duchesses brings me a little closer to understanding the home that was as much theirs as it is mine.

OPPOSITE *King Henry VIII*, after Holbein.
TOP *The Marquis of Granby and Lady Elizabeth Manners as Children with Dogs, Turk and Crab*, 1772, by Sir Joshua Reynolds.
ABOVE *Turk*, 1778, by George Stubbs.

OPPOSITE ABOVE *The Proverbs*, by David Teniers the Younger.
OPPOSITE BELOW *Hollandia*, 1692, by William van de Velde II.
LEFT ABOVE *Woodcutter's Home, c.*1780, by Thomas Gainsborough.
LEFT BELOW *The Grace before Meat* (also known as *Prayer Before the Meal*), by Jan Steen.
BELOW *Violet, Duchess of Rutland*, 1889, by Sir James Jebusa Shannon. (This now hangs on the 40-Acre Landing.)

THE KING'S ROOMS

IT IS NO COINCIDENCE that many of the main bedrooms are on the second floor. One of Elizabeth's main reasons for rebuilding the low Charles II castle was to add another storey so that she could fully appreciate the superb views. But, surprisingly, she chose the least pleasing aspect for the King's Rooms. The windows look out over the porte cochère, and the north-east and north-west towers block most of a fairly dull view over the flat part of the Vale. Eller wrote that the 5th Duke had even considered converting the suite into a library. Thankfully he didn't and so we have some idea of what the Prince Regent, and later Queen Victoria, experienced when they stayed here. Slept in very rarely in the years after the Second World War, all these rooms are now used as guest bedrooms again.

The King's Sitting Room is lined in exquisite Chinese wallpaper. The day bed, with its mahogany canopy dressed in yellow silk damask, is by Gillow. The secretaire by the London cabinet-makers Vile and Cobb, c.1760, is one of the most important pieces of furniture we have and is due to be restored. The date suggests it could have been here since the 3rd Duke's time but little else is known about it.

RIGHT Elizabeth devised these rooms so that they would be suitable for Royal visitors. Her hand was sure. The King's Rooms remain the most intact suite in the castle and, despite the disappointing outlook, our visitors seem to find them charming. In the Sitting Room, shown here, there is a Vile and Cobb secretaire-cabinet in the left-hand corner.
BELOW LEFT The anthemion, or palmette, motif on the cornice on the day bed canopy in the Sitting Room looks like fanned peacock feathers from a distance; it also appears above the half-tester bed in the Bedroom and above the day bed in the Dressing Room.
BELOW RIGHT The head of Mercury, carved by M. Bogaert, on a bookcase by Morel and Hughes, c.1810.

Violet opened up a new doorway from the Picture Gallery into the King's Sitting Room. As usual, she noted her reasons: '*That room cannot be used as a separate room – for want of said door. I should try to get it on the right side of the fireplace – not for big things to pass, but just one person at a time.*' Her wish was granted. These days a suite of three rooms, as well as a lavatory and a bathroom, with only one access point would probably not pass fire or health and safety regulations anyway. Violet also added a lavatory, with which she was very pleased, to this room. She notes: '*We also built out a turret to get a lavatory for this suite – great success (me and Mr Mearing) with Henry's consent.*' She added, '*This room can be turned into a young ladies bedroom and for that purpose I have placed an Italian table and a washstand.*'

The King's Bedroom is fractionally smaller than the Sitting Room but outshines its neighbour with the splendour of Gillow's bed with its carved mahogany pillars. The yellow silk damask of the bed and the seating matches that in the other two rooms. Aunt Ursie remembers yellow silk being found, wrapped up in brown paper and tied with string, in the Carpenter's Workshop when she was a girl. Presumably Violet used that, but my mother-in-law replaced the silk, at least on the seating, in the 1980s, making a special trip to Paris to buy it.

BELOW LEFT A pair of herons painted on the early 19th-century Chinese wallpaper in the King's Sitting Room.

BELOW RIGHT A double jib door cut into the corner of the Sitting Room leads to the lavatory that Violet was so proud to have added in the early 1900s.

RIGHT The mahogany and parcel-gilt tester bedstead in the King's Bedroom was supplied by Gillow in c.1821, five years after the rooms had had to be rebuilt and redecorated following the fire. I added the red bedspread, which is a modern Indian sari.

OVERLEAF The rosewood and ebony parcel-gilt and lacquer wardrobe in the King's Bedroom is attributed to Morel and Hughes and dates from c.1810; there is a pair in the Wellington Room.

Violet's greatest achievement in the King's Rooms was the introduction of plumbing to the bathroom. '*This I am proud of – Mr Mearing carried out all my ideas very well.*' It draws many admiring visitors. There are two stories about the hollowed-out wall of the narrow corridor leading to the recessed space for the Royal ablutions: one is that it was done to allow the Prince Regent to squeeze his ever-expanding girth through the space; the other is that it was done to ease the way for Edward VII, who was short but had particularly wide shoulders.

Like the King's Sitting Room and Bedroom, the Dressing Room is decorated in intricately painted Chinese wallpaper, and the yellow silk and gilded cornice of the day bed match those of the other rooms. The bed and the loveseat are probably by Gillow. What appears to be a trible mahogany wardrobe in the Dressing Room actually conceals access to the bathroom as well as a built-in cupboard.

The 3rd Duke was responsible for buying the painting of *The Temptation of Anthony* by David Teniers the Younger that hangs here. It cost him £13 13s. in 1747.

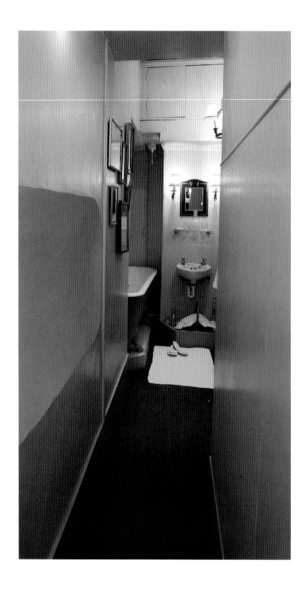

LEFT The wall on the left of the passage that leads to the bathroom from the King's Bathroom was scooped out to enable Royal visitors with large stomachs or wide shoulders to negotiate the space more easily. The plumbing was added by Violet in the early 1900s.
RIGHT The original way to the bathroom was through one of the doors in the maghogany wardrobe of the Dressing Room. The parcel-gilt and ebonized cradle with an oval basket and swan neck finial is French and was given to Elizabeth, the 5th Duchess, by the Prince Regent on the birth of one of her children.

THE EARL'S LANDING

THE EARL'S LANDING runs between the King's Rooms and the Regent's Gallery at the top of the cantilevered Grand Staircase. These stairs are an exact copy of the ones that crumbled to dust in the intense heat of the fire. Someone allegedly bricked up the doorway into the Regent's Gallery from here to stop the flames from spreading further. Other than providing access to the Picture Gallery and the Libraries, the landing serves no aesthetic function except to exhibit the portraits of the eight Earls of Rutland painted in the mid-1670s as a set of ancestors by the Anglo-Flemish artist Jeremiah van der Eyden, who had at one stage worked in Peter Lely's studio. This instant ancestry was the impulse of the 9th Earl of Rutland and parallels the set of Scottish kings at Holyroodhouse, suggesting that it was perhaps a fashion at the time. He showed surprisingly bad taste in artists when, for his own portrait, he commissioned Johann Baptist Closterman, who was the less successful brother of the far more talented Johann Closterman, Kneller's greatest rival in the late 17th and early 18th centuries.

BELOW The Earl's Landing is named for its display of portraits of all the Earls by Jeremiah van der Eyden in the mid-1670s. RIGHT The Earl's Staircase, rebuilt after the fire, leads up to the Regent's Gallery, which was saved from the flames by someone bricking up the doorway.

THE REGENT'S GALLERY

A GALLERY, in the same location and of roughly the same proportions as the present one, existed in the Charles II castle. Under Elizabeth's sway its length of 131 feet remained the same, but its width of 17 feet 8 inches was doubled in the centre section when it was extended into Wyatt's new Round Tower (which was then renamed during a visit from the Prince Regent). In this bowed section of the room are five windows, each nearly 14 feet high, which frame views of the Rose Garden and the village of Knipton beyond.

The gallery was used in the early 20th century as a general living room with breakfast, luncheon and tea being served in here. Violet mentions that the little library was the serving room. Today it is purely a gallery again and used for occasional parties and music recitals.

LEFT The central, wide, section of the Regent's Gallery contains most of the seating furniture, including the ottoman that Violet brought here from the Guard Room; she said its needlepoint was 'worked on by the ladies of the family'. The Regency gilt side chairs around the circular table in the centre are by Elward Marsh & Tatham. They were reupholstered by David's grandmother Kakoo using material bought using coupons saved up during the Second World War. The glass dome on the table contains a 19th-century carved alabaster model of the Warwick vase.
BELOW Looking towards the huge looking glass on the end wall that separates the Regent's Gallery from the Chapel. Most of the busts are by Joseph Nollekens.
OVERLEAF The windows have their original elaborate Regency pelmets, but the red damask curtains were replaced in the early 1990s by my mother-in-law. All the material that was still intact was salvaged, and I have used it to recover the giltwood sofas.

We repainted the room in 2007 after David had taken his penknife to the walls to scrape away layers of paint to reveal the original colour. At the same time, there was a great family debate as to whether or not we should keep the carpet. There were two camps of thought: one, which included me, thought the room would look better without it, while the other, which included David, believed that as it was made for the room, it should stay. David's camp won and it is being restored. It dates from the 1840s when the room was refurnished, which ties in with Queen Victoria's visit in 1843. Annabel Westman explained that the floral pattern is typical of the fashion at the time.

Waterford crystal chandeliers, gilded mirrors and three fireplaces add to the splendour of this room. One riddle, however, remains unsolved. It is extraordinary but no seems to know when the enormous looking glass, which covers the entire wall that divides the Gallery from the Chapel, was put in. Eller describes a folding door from the Regent's Gallery through which the Chapel altarpiece could be seen 160 feet away from the back of the room. Violet notes that she must put a very heavy stone-coloured velveteen curtain at the Chapel door on the turret stairs to keep the draught out. After that, there is no mention of a door connecting these two great rooms. Maybe Janetta, the second wife of the 7th Duke, was responsible for putting in the looking glass before Violet arrived and therefore Violet didn't feel the need to write about it?

Eller wrote: '*The Regent's Gallery was never completed in its decorations; and with the exception of some richly designed cabinets, and three splendid chandeliers of cut glass, there is a great plainness in the furniture.*' The furniture here now is by various makers but a pair of sofas by Morel and Hughes of *c.*1810 and carved by Bogaerts with rosettes, honeysuckle and other ornaments

LEFT One of the Regent's Gallery's Gobelin tapestries hangs above a Louis XVI ebony and Boulle marquetry breakfront display cabinet that was bought by the 5th Duke and Duchess on their visit to Paris in 1814 from the shop belonging to Monsieur Mallerondts and Monsieur Coquilles. The bust on the left is of the Marquis of Granby, by Joseph Nollekens, and the one on the right is of Elizabeth, by Matthew Cotes Wyatt.
RIGHT A detail from the Gobelin tapestries.

were, according to the invoice in the archives, for Elizabeth's Drawing Room (later the Elizabeth Saloon).

The most impressive attraction in here is the Don Quixote tapestries acquired by the 5th Duke in Paris in 1814. They were originally a gift from Louis XVI to the Comte de Saint-Florentin, Marquis de la Vrillière, in 1770. He displayed them during the autumn and winter months in his hôtel in Paris (now the American Embassy), alternating them with taffeta hanging in the summer.[16] The series of 28 different subjects was designed by Charles-Antoine Coypel for the Gobelins tapestry workshop in Paris, mostly between 1714 and 1734, the last scene being delivered in 1751.[17] In October 1752, the director of the Gobelins workshop noted: 'One advantage of this series of hangings is that it can be separated into as many or as few

pieces as desired, and is consequently more convenient for the King to present to Princes or Ambassadors.'

The hangings continued in production until the French Revolution with nine sets being woven in total. The subjects remained unchanged but the large borders or *alentours* were altered with each weaving but always with a peacock design in the centre at the top, coincidentally an essential part of the Manners crest. Most of the tapestries have yellow backgrounds – the crimson was introduced later. The tapestries in the gallery, with their Dubarry pink and crimson grounds, are part of the eighth series. Two of the tapestries are signed 'Audran', and one 'Cozette', the weavers of this particular series.

When they were first made they would have been full of sumptuous colours and incidental detail. Eller commented

on the '*brilliancy of colouring*', which has sadly faded, but the light-hearted imagery and fine draughtsmanship can still be seen in the scenes, and in the floral garlands, animals and other decorative details.

One person who didn't agree was Violet. '*If I were rich, the tapestries should be entirely surrounded by white marble – the pink it seems to me is given an especially lovely tone by it – (most people have French boiseries of fawn coloured wood against their sets).*' She added, even more alarmingly: '*But I think they ought to be sold for a huge sum – to help death duties and then I would place the two Cheveley cabinets (the ones in our private drawing room) with just china in them in the spaces on either side of centre mantelpiece and perhaps I would put Shannon pictures here and keep the Hoppner's over the mantlepieces.*'

Tim Knox was surprised at the number of Nollekens busts here, joking that the castle was 'simply infested with them'. Eller counts 13 '*in various parts of the gallery, and principally on marble columns*'. Tim explained that Joseph Nollekens was the most successful portrait sculptor of the late 18th century. The busts that we have here, all sculpted from life, include portraits of the Prince Regent, William Pitt the Younger (a friend of the 4th Duke), the 5th Duke and Duchess and George II. There are also busts of the Marquis of Granby and Admiral Keppel by Giuseppe Ceracci, and of William Pitt the Elder by Joseph Wilton.

The painting of Elizabeth that hangs above the fireplace was started by John Hoppner and finished by Matthew Cotes Wyatt. She is shown in her favourite flower garden leaning against a column, which is inscribed with the following:

One cultivated spot behold, which spreads
Its flowery blossom to the noon tide beam,
Where numerous rosebuds rear their blushing heads,
And poppies gay, and fragrant violets teem.

Far from the busy world's unceasing sound
Here has Eliza fixed her favourite seat,
Chaste emblem of the tranquil scene around,
Pure as the flower which smiles beneath her feet.

The portrait of the Duchess of Somerset by William Hogarth is of particular family interest because it is through the marriage of her daughter Lady Frances Seymour to the Marquis of Granby in 1750 that Cheveley Park passed to the Rutlands.

OPPOSITE LEFT A detail of one of the Regency giltwood sofas by Morel and Hughes, *c*.1810.

OPPOSITE CENTRE The Cat's Cradle, an early 19th-century board game, on a painted stand.

OPPOSITE RIGHT A detail of one of the boulle cabinets with a pretty display of china, the provenance of which is unknown.

ABOVE A marble group of *The Three Graces*, after Antonio Canova, from the first half of the 19th century.

RIGHT A marble bust of the 5th Duke by Joseph Nollekens, *c*.1780, placed in front of the looking-glass wall that reflects the length of the gallery.

THE LIBRARIES

SIR JOHN THOROTON designed both the large and the small library in his trademark Gothic style after the fire. The bigger of the two rooms has a superb faux wooden ceiling, quite different to the dramatic vaulted effects in other rooms he created. It is decorated with the family coats of arms in each corner: Manners impaling Howard, Beaufort, Somerset and Sutton. Eller argued against the common view that the room was gloomy with its view overlooking the courtyard and the Central and Flag Towers. He wrote: '*I cannot appreciate this objection as at all applicable to a room, the very design of which is, to concentrate the attention within its walls, rather than permit a diversion of the thoughts to external beauties.*' It was an opinion not shared by Violet,

LEFT The main library probably looks very much as it did in Violet's time; certainly the furniture is largely as she described it. The new arrival is the leather elephant which I gave to David on his 40th birthday. The picture above the fireplace is *The 5th Duke of Rutland*, by Francis Grant.

ABOVE The Manners' arms impaled with those of the Sutton family on the library ceiling.

ABOVE LEFT Seen across the Courtyard from a Library window is the clock on the Flag Tower, built by James Wyatt.

ABOVE CENTRE Violet added the heating and seats under the windows. We found the pretty box in one of the towers. It was badly damaged, which is probably why it had been put there, but we have since restored it.

ABOVE RIGHT Shelves of books that have been cleaned and catalogued by NADFAS.

OPPOSITE Looking through to the smaller library with the billiard table. Next to the globe is the metamorphic chair which has always been a great source of fascination for young children as it stretches out to form library steps.

who wrote: 'The outlook is ugly!' She described the bookcases almost filling the windows and so she cleared these to improve the light, created window seats on which to look at books and installed heating.

Her pronouncement is justified. The attractive Gothic-shaped windows, with carved and gilded flowers and fruit, are the only redeeming features of the whole aspect and could explain why, given its position, Thoroton chose to design a cosy room with a low ceiling. Or maybe it was merely a cheaper option for a room that was already inferior by comparison to its neighbours.

The wallpaper, from the Zoffany Archive collection, was hung by my mother-in-law, who took David with her to choose it. Among the assortment of furniture and desks around the room now is a metamorphic library armchair reputedly made by Gillow. If you release a catch on the back of the chair and ease the seat forwards, the mechanism reverses to display a neat set of library steps. I have bought more soft furnishings from London salerooms recently to replace, or as alternatives to, previously worn or uncomfortable chairs and sofas.

The portrait of the 5th Duke by Francis Grant above the fireplace was presented to the Duke by his tenants in 1856 as a mark of their respect and appreciation. Violet wrote, 'I must wait – or perhaps a generation better pass – before moving the awful picture by Sir F Grant RA – of the 5th Duke at 80 years old – given him by tenants who will then be dead.'

On the top of the numbered oak bookcases are a set of eight bronzed plaster busts of emperors and philosophers, including Homer and Demosthenes. Eller writes: 'a marble slab runs the whole extent of the top of the bookcases for busts and other

articles of vertu.' I think it is safe to assume that the present busts are the ones he was referring to but the '*other articles of vertu*' are unknown. The library also contains a very fine pair of terrestrial and celestial Regency globes on grained stands by J. & W. Cary, widely considered to be the greatest British globe-makers of the late Georgian period.

The bookcases are in two sections and line both sides and ends of the room. The lower half, with locks, contain, Eller wrote, '*such literary treasures as require careful and infrequent handling, such as MSS., original drawings by the great masters, illustrated works, and valuable editions of standard writers*'. The 9th Duke, however, spent a lot of time cataloguing the contents and the more valuable items were removed. The upper half of the cases are for the books.

The varied reading matter that has been accumulated over the last 550 years includes titles on divinity, classics and illustrated works and totals nearly

8,000 volumes. The earliest are French religious manuscripts of the Divine Office, which date back to 1457. Volunteers from NADFAS are cleaning and cataloguing the whole collection and expect the job to take sixteen years. They have already been here for eight.

The small library was created by Violet and her son the 9th Duke as a smaller version of its big brother. Matching the marble on the bookcase ledges with the big library was impossible so they improvised and settled for a different material. Above the fireplace there is a very austere picture of Janetta, the second wife of the 7th Duke. The varied titles of the sham books for the jib door that leads to Violet's Corridor were compiled by Charlie Anglesey, the 9th Duke's brother-in-law, and include Homer's *Iliad*, Izaak Walton's *The Compleat Angler*, Swift's *Works*, Pope's *Essays* and *Fables de la Fontaine*. How or why he chose them is anyone's guess.

OPPOSITE BELOW The small library has been used as a billiard room, a serving room for meals and a sealed chamber for the National Archives during the Second World War. It is now a billiard room again.
OPPOSITE ABOVE A section of the mantelpiece that Violet notes was made up from one belonging to Mr Marlay, the 8th Duke's maternal uncle.
BELOW LEFT The jib door was made to look like book shelves using just the spines of the books.
BELOW RIGHT A globe on a George IV circular bookstand, c.1825.

THE CHAPEL AND OUTER CHAPEL

A CHAPEL occupied this site in the Charles II castle but Wyatt embellished it in the Gothic manner. Today it is approached via an oak Gothic-style door at the top of a stone staircase leading down from the Regent's Gallery. Interestingly, an old bricked-up doorway on the ground floor on an outside wall suggests there was once separate access for staff and tenants. There are two private family balconies: one at the back and one above the altar. My late father-in-law told me how, as a boy, he once hid in the private vantage point at the back during a service and made paper aeroplanes to 'bomb' his brother Roger who was sitting below.

The Chapel seats a congregation of up to 50 members in total, although sadly not on the pews of Elizabeth's day; for some reason those finished up at Bottesford Church, where they remain. Ironically, we are to be the grateful

BELOW LEFT Looking through the Gothic archways from the Chapel to the outer chapel where there is an effigy of a medieval abbot, which was excavated by the 9th Duke.

BELOW RIGHT *The Holy Family with the Infant St John*, by Bartolomé Esteban Murillo, hangs above the altar.

RIGHT The aisle floor is black marble; the wood floor on either side would have been mostly hidden by the original pews. Violet added the wrought-iron screen.

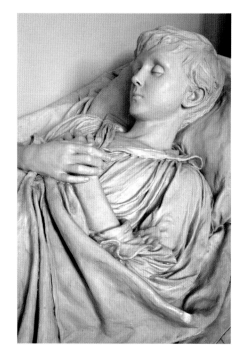

recipients of some other older pews that the church wants to replace (again sadly, not the original ones).

Our family chaplain, the Revd Stuart Forster, is also Rector of Bottesford, and he takes regular services in the Chapel. All our children have been christened here and the harvest festival and Christmas carol services are annual social events. The estate's own male voice choir, the Belvoir Wassailers, makes full use of the excellent acoustics during rehearsals for the 'Belvoir by Candlelight' concerts at Christmas.

Hanging over the altar is a painting that is the most important example of the Italian and Spanish Schools at Belvoir, *The Holy Family with the Infant St John,* mid-17th century, by Bartolomé Esteban Murillo. Murillo, a native of Seville, was greatly loved by English collectors in the 18th century; this is surprising considering that the majority of

ABOVE LEFT Carved peacocks decorate the pews that were originally in the Chapel but are now in Bottesford Church.
ABOVE CENTRE A plaster bust of Lady Diana Manners, c.1910, by her mother Violet, Duchess of Rutland, just outside the outer chapel.
ABOVE RIGHT A plaster cast of Lord Haddon, the elder brother of the 9th Duke, who died aged nine, by his mother, Violet, Duchess of Rutland. It was exhibited in the Tate Gallery.

his works are of a deeply Catholic nature, painted during the period of the Counter Reformation. However, his depiction of the Holy Family in the guise of simple Spanish peasants, more domestic than triumphant, and his charming genre scenes of daily life were instantly popular and sought-after in England. The colouring of our picture, greatly admired down the years, and its superb condition have caused to it be described as the greatest of Murillo's works in England, finer even than the similar work in the Wallace Collection. It was bought in Madrid with two other works by the same artist by Colonel William Stanhope, later the 1st Earl of Harrington, while he was British Ambassador to Spain between 1721 and 1727. Harrington's grandson, the 3rd Earl, who was at Eton with the 4th Duke of Rutland and served as his Commander-in-Chief in Ireland while the 4th Duke was Lord Lieutenant, sold them to the Duke, who paid £1,500 for the three – but not without a valuation from a trio of experts including the ubiquitous Joshua Reynolds.

The finely sculpted recumbent figure to the left of the altar is the finished plaster cast of the nine-year-old Lord Haddon, modelled by his grieving mother Violet soon after his death. There is a marble version in the Chapel at Haddon Hall.

Hanging on the walls of the chapel and outer chapel are three Mortlake tapestries, after cartoons by Raphael, depicting episodes from the New Testament from the lives of St Peter and St Paul: 'Christ's Charge to Peter', 'The Death of Ananias' and 'Elymas Struck with Blindness'. The cartoons, now in the Victoria and Albert Museum, London, were originally commissioned from Raphael in 1515 by Pope Leo X as designs for tapestries to hang in the Sistine Chapel in Rome. In 1623 seven of the original ten cartoons were purchased by Charles I for copying at Mortlake and they proved to be the most popular subjects woven by the factory. At least five subjects were supplied to Belvoir for a total cost of £230 15s. by Philip Hollinberch in 1653–4, one of the leading weavers at Mortlake.

A rather touching plaque has been fastened to the organ, reading: 'This organ was presented to the Belvoir Castle Chapel by Sir George Manners to commemorate all the happy times since 1867.' Sir George was a grandson of the 5th Duke and Duchess (his maternal grandparents were the 13th Duke and Duchess of Norfolk). We haven't found out what the significance of 1867 is except that he would have been seven years old and may have been allowed to sit in the chapel from that age. The organ was erected in 1937, two years before he died aged 79. The visitors' books show

that he was a regular visitor and he lived at Little Haddon Hall in Suffolk.

Robert de Todeni's tomb, which is in the outer chapel, was excavated from the site of the old Belvoir Priory (now the site of the Dower House) in 1726. An iron box close to the tomb was discovered buried in front of the cannonade (the bastion overlooking the castle approach), filled with 17th-century musket balls, probably from the Civil War. The recumbent effigies of the early medieval monks which now lie in the outer chapel were excavated by the 9th Duke on the site of Croxton Priory, part of the Belvoir estate, during the 1920s.

ABOVE LEFT The Chapel organ was presented to the family by Sir George Manners, a grandson of the 5th Duke and Duchess.
ABOVE CENTRE The tomb of Robert de Todeni is now in the outer chapel.
ABOVE RIGHT Another effigy of a medieval abbot excavated by the 9th Duke in 1923 – one of several in the outer chapel.
OVERLEAF This Mortlake tapestry from a cartoon by Raphael depicts 'Christ's Charge to Peter' (which was to 'Feed my Sheep').

THE KITCHENS AND BEER CELLARS

THE WYATTS designed the cavernous kitchens for Elizabeth's household in the basement of the south-west wing. Huge mullioned windows let in plenty of light and the face of the clock tower peering on to proceedings would have left no excuse for lateness. The game larders are just outside in the inner courtyard.

The whole kitchen area served as a single integrated unit with extensive larders and a scullery on the cool northern wall while, to the south, lie a pastry room and bedrooms for the cook and kitchen maids. A serving hatch to the south facilitated the Duke's private Dining Room and the north hatch served the State Dining Room. The Stewards' Dining Room, now our public restaurant, seated up to 100 and was used by the senior staff while the junior ones used the Servants' Hall.

Each dining room ate from separate menus. Vast quantities of food were consumed, and detailed records were listed in the cooks' books. Between

OPPOSITE One of the two kitchen ranges installed by Briffault of London, c.1900, with copper water pans. The kitchen was last used in 1940.

BELOW A huge copper hood was fitted over the roasting range and spit. At the far end of the room is another range, by J. Moritt & Sons of Newark. Just in front of it is Violet's sculpting bench with its revolving top which was brought into the kitchen before the First World War to use as a carving gadget.

December 1839 and April 1840, the kitchen used 3,333 loaves of bread, 22,963 pounds of meat, 2,589 head of game and numerous other ingredients in order to supply 1,997 people at the Duke's table, 2,241 in the Stewards' Room and 11, 312 in the Servants' Hall, Nursery and Kitchens. Seventy hogsheads (about 28,000 pints) of ale and 200 dozen bottles of wine were drunk.

In 1900, the French cook, Louis Thevenot, was the highest paid member of the entire Rutland household. His salary of £140 a year, plus £15 12s. allowances for personal beer and laundry costs, represents about £60,000 by today's standards. He was responsible for devising fresh menus every day, subject to the Duchess's approval. He had a small, effective and efficient female staff comprising Florence Randall as head kitchen maid earning £35 per annum, Mary Reynolds as second kitchen maid on £22 per

annum and Sarah Thompson, the scullery maid, taking home £18 per annum. Today we run one large commercial kitchen in a space behind the Stewards' Restaurant, with about half the number of staff.

Copper pans above the enormous copper hood over the spit, cooking ranges made by different manufacturers (Briffault, John Briant of Hereford, J. Moritt & Sons of Newark), hot closets and boilers are all typical features of a kitchen for this period. An unlikely appliance is Violet's sculpture bench, with revolving top. It was moved to the kitchen before the First World War as an unexpected but welcome gadget for carving large joints of meat.

The housekeeper and her stillroom maid made pastries and cakes for the family in the Stillroom, where jams, jellies and ice cream were made and fruit preserved in bottles too. It has not changed since the 1820s and still houses the pastry oven made by T. Powell of Leicester Square, London. Other utensils include a marble pestle and mortar for grinding sugar, marzipan and so on, a zinc-lined box for storing ice and all manner of moulds and baking equipment.

Beer was brewed in the brewhouse in Belvoir village until the end of the 19th century and stored in three castle beer cellars under what is now the Stewards' Restaurant. The first

LEFT The Pastry Room, designed by James Wyatt shortly before 1813. It is dressed much as it would have looked during the 1820s.
ABOVE LEFT Among items of kitchen equipment on the window sill is a knife sharpener on the right that is still in use today.
ABOVE CENTRE The original Pastry Room door sign.
ABOVE RIGHT Drawers in the Pastry Room were designed for spices and other provisions.

contained 28 barrels, the second held 1,099 hogsheads in 11 vessels, each containing about 48 hogsheads. The barrels and vats in today's No.1 cellar are between 150 and 200 years old. Reproductions of photographs on the wall taken in about 1880 show the immense size of the barrel known as Robert de Todeni: it contained 1,300 gallons. A label attached to it with the date 'May 16th, 1815' was the Marquis of Granby's birth date and the day the barrel was filled with beer. It was tapped for his coming of age.

Allegedly, Belvoir's apprentice coopers (barrel-makers) were rolled down the hill inside their first barrel. If it survived intact they qualified and were rewarded with a pint of beer and a pork pie; if the barrel broke they remained an apprentice.

LEFT In the Courtyard, below the Flag Tower – seen here with the family flag flying on top – are the circular game larders. These are now home to our Harris hawks which regularly patrol the pigeon population on the roofs.
RIGHT Original beer barrels dating from the time when the estate brewed its own beer, stand in the beer cellars.

Our Private Apartments

THE PRIVATE SIDE OF THE HOUSE is made up of a self-contained flat on the first floor and some guest bedrooms, immediately above it on the second floor, which had been used by the family before we moved in. The first-floor rooms were an obvious place for us to create a home because they were the only vacant space large enough to house a growing family, and were central for accessing both the private and public sides of the house. Our first major job was to put in a kitchen and make a family playroom or television room, so giving a heart to our space and a centre for our family life.

OPPOSITE The south-east-facing side of the castle contains our private apartments and overlooks the Kitchen Garden, designed by James Wyatt.
BELOW The division between the public rooms and our private, family apartments is all too clear when you look down from the Ballroom Stairs on to the screen that separates them.

WELLINGTON'S APARTMENTS

THESE ARE NAMED after the Duke of Wellington, who was a close personal friend of the 5th Duke and slept here on the frequent occasions that he was a house guest. His bedroom in the north-east tower, under the Elizabeth Saloon, is now our television room. His dressing room has become our kitchen, and an adjoining room is our bedroom.

I first thought that it might be difficult to use these rooms, as we would have to use a corridor that was part of a landing on the public route. Apart from wanting to avoid any potentially embarrassing situations, it was only fair to protect our visitors from seeing bicycles, footballs, pushchairs and Barbie dolls. However, the Works Department came up with a clever solution and made a shaped screen that allows the light from the Ballroom Stairs into the corridor but shields the mess.

BELOW The area outside our kitchen and television room was once part of the Duke of Wellington's suite of rooms. Now it seems to be a breeding ground for school pictures, pet portraits and toys.
RIGHT The semi-circular room in the north-east tower – once a bedroom that the Duke of Wellington and, later, Violet used – is now our cosy television room.

After Wellington slept in the bedroom, various occupants, including Violet, who used it from 1916, enjoyed its curved ceiling and woke up to views of rolling countryside, over the Vale of Belvoir to Lincoln Cathedral (on a clear day). Then Janetta, the second wife of the 7th Duke, moved the Duke of Wellington's bed and some of the furniture upstairs to what had been known as the Ambassadors' Room; once honoured with the bed, it was renamed the Wellington Room. Wellington had been dead for ten years by the time Janetta married and maybe she thought that this extended suite was an unnecessary monument to an old friend. We are not sure what she used the rooms for, but by the 9th Duke's time, they had become

nurseries. This is where Nanny Webb looked after her charges. She died in 1978 after 54 years of service, having brought up my father-in-law's generation as well as my husband and his siblings. Before we could do anything the historic Crace wallpaper that Violet had hung here had to be professionally removed and stored away. Who knows how other generations may want to use this space? The built-in cupboard, which was once Wellington's wardrobe in his dressing room, now provides storage for toys in our kitchen. It was made by Gillow; Elizabeth was a long way ahead of her time in building cupboards into recesses.

Because our bedroom is next door to the one that was Wellington's, we wonder whether Wellington's mistress,

Mrs Arbuthnot, slept here. There are no visitors' books for that period but it would have been interesting to see how many times she stayed at Belvoir at the same time as he did. We do know that our bedroom was used by the 5th Duke during Queen Victoria's visit in 1843, presumably to allow the members of the Royal party more privacy by having a whole floor to themselves. And latterly it was David's nursery. He remembers it with lino-covered floors and a Belling stove in the corner that re-heated the children's food which, having come up from the downstairs kitchen, had become cold.

My mother-in-law hung the wallpaper, and had had the curtains made not long before we moved in. I was lucky

OPPOSITE AND BELOW Our family kitchen, once a dressing room to its neighbouring bedroom, is remembered by David as Nanny Webb's room. The fireplace is fitted into the curved wall of the north-east tower. Mark Wilkinson designed the kitchen units to fit in with the room's proportions. Since we closed the old kitchen downstairs, needing it for office space, all the family cooking – from family breakfasts to formal dinners – has been done here. It is hive of activity all day, especially in the school holidays when the children like to help out.

BELOW LEFT When we moved into the castle, there was a brass bed in our bedroom, but I felt that the room needed something grander – and more comfortable. Our Works Department came up trumps and made the bed using a pair of bedposts, presumed to be by Gillow, that we found in the Engine Yard on the estate. I just had the headboard and hangings made to match the existing window curtains.

BELOW RIGHT The dressing table, like the bedposts, is thought to be by Gillow and could well be the one that Violet describes as '*common*' in her notebook. The portrait above the cheval looking glass is of Elizabeth Drake, the 3rd Duke's common-law wife, 1747, by Johann Rudolf Studer of Basle.

that the material that she used, by Colefax & Fowler, was still in production, so we could have bed hangings made to match. The Axminster carpet with its red-brick and green tones was salvaged from storage. Our room is a shortcut to the kitchen from the Staunton Tower lobby and takes some traffic from friends and family wandering through to the kitchen to find us, but the carpet is wearing well. Although our bedroom isn't in an ideal position, I wanted to be close to our young children; we may move to a more private room when they are older.

The spectacular Boulle commode in our bathroom is far too good to be in there. But it was in storage in Nanny Webb's old room when we first looked round these rooms and, although it needs a lot of restoration, it is too nice to be tucked away. It is possibly the one listed in a bill of 27 December 1811 from Thomas Partners – 'to repair and polish a Boulle brass inlaid tortoiseshell veneered rectangular commode circa 1710' – which was once in the Regent's Gallery.

The lobby and corridor that link these and our children's rooms used to be known as the Egyptian Corridor; I sometimes wonder whether the 9th Duke named it – he was a regular visitor to Egypt and may have displayed mementoes here. It is, admittedly, dark because the small windows with an outlook on to an

LEFT I bought the Victorian oval mirror for our bathroom from a sale in Herefordshire. It is reflecting *The Death of Actaeon*, 1777, by Sir Joshua Reynolds' friend Angelica Kauffman. The 4th Duke gave this picture to his mother-in-law, the Duchess of Beaufort, who left it to her daughter Mary Isabella, the 4th Duchess. I moved it into our bathroom from the Egyptian Corridor.

RIGHT A detail of the badly damaged Boulle commode in our bathroom.

BELOW LEFT Portraits of the Boyle sisters, members of a local family, hang above the lavatory.

BELOW RIGHT The view from our bathroom door looks across a corridor and David's dressing room to our daughter Eliza's room.

enclosed courtyard let in little natural light. The rather dour subject matter of many of the pictures adds to the gloom. There is a painted iron tray depicting the death from tetanus of Captain Lord Robert Manners, which the 9th Duke bought in February 1914 from Hamilton Mee for £20 (see page 100), a fairly graphic picture of the Belvoir Hounds killing a fox by John Sartorius, and an unknown artist's vision of a tiger attacking a cossack. Until very recently these were accompanied by *The Death of Actaeon,* 1777, by Angelica Kauffman, which now hangs in our bathroom.

On a more cheerful note, there is also a portrait of David painted by our friend Simon Hopkins, which was part of my wedding present to David, and a portrait of me by Sergi Pavlenko, which my father-in-law commissioned in 1996 after our first two children were born. And at the end of the corridor, outside the Staunton Tower, is a picture of the 6th Duke's favourite hunters and dogs by John Ferneley, a former coach painter for the 5th Duke, who encouraged Ferneley to become apprenticed to another local artist, Ben Marshall.

LEFT *The 11th Duchess of Rutland, 1998*, by Sergi Pavlenko.
BELOW *The 11th Duke of Rutland, 1992*, by Simon Hopkins.
BOTTOM The 6th Duke's favourite hunters and dogs, by John Ferneley. The Duke commissioned this painting in 1857 shortly before he took over the mastership of the Belvoir Hounds in 1860.

FAR LEFT The gloomy Egyptian Corridor, lit only by one window from the archway, and two overhanging lights. Many of the pictures are portraits by Sir Peter Lely.
LEFT ABOVE Our sons Charles and Hugo chose the bloodthirsty picture of a *Siberian Tiger Attacking a Cossack*, by an unknown artist, from the picture storeroom because they liked it.
LEFT BELOW *Two Girls with a Jay in a Cage* by the Revd M. W. Peters. The Revd Peters was keeper of the 5th Duke's art collection until he came of age. He lived in our old home, Knipton Lodge, on the edge of the park.

THE STAUNTON TOWER – THE FAMILY CELLAR

ROBERT DE TODENI built the Staunton Tower as the first castle's stronghold. It was named after the local landowner who was its guard. The Wars of the Roses left the first castle in ruins until the 1st Earl of Rutland rebuilt it between 1528 and 1543. Our curiously named cellar – it is not in the cellar at all but on the second floor of the tower – dates back to this period, so far as anyone can tell, and it is possible that some parts of it could date from the 15th century or perhaps even earlier. One thing is certain: it is the oldest part of the castle.

The stone vaulted interior is intersected with eight plain bevelled ribs from the floor that meet in a point on the ceiling which is capped with a boss marked with the letter M. The cellar is divided into bins, which together are capable of holding 16,750 bottles. The temperature is held at half a degree either side of 56°F all through the year. The children's Christmas stockings are stored in here on Christmas Eve because it's the nearest hiding place to their bedrooms.

LEFT ABOVE The 'M' on the ceiling boss possibly stands for Manners.
LEFT CENTRE On a bracket shelf in the cellar is a wood carving featuring a peacock. No one knows quite what the piece is, but it looks Indian and may have been a gift.
LEFT BELOW Wine and champagne for shoot dinners are stored here.
ABOVE Wine bins surround a table used to store table linen.
RIGHT Wine that was on the HMS *Resolution*, on which Lord Robert Manners died in 1782.

THE PRIVATE DINING ROOM

ELIZABETH USED THIS ROOM as her private dining room, as have the generations since; it is still a long way from the kitchen, so a kitchenette has been added in the next room. When I first read Eller's notes on the pictures that were in here, I was puzzled. He writes that the Stubbs landscapes originally hung here. However, they are too big to fit inside the moulded panels on the walls. Violet's notebook revealed the explanation.

After improving the private Drawing Room she decided to make another '*very ugly*' room into a '*Charles II room*' to display the many Lely portraits dotted about the castle. A shop in Rathbone Place in London made the panels to her specification and she instructed Ricketts of Belvoir, a father-and-son business that had worked on the Drawing Room, to position and fix them. She adds: '*A man from Woolsthorpe,*

ABOVE The mahogany sideboard and wine cooler were made by William Wilkinson in 1808 to a design by J. J. Boileau in order to fit exactly into the curve of the alcove in the end wall. The Queen Anne mirror was hung above it by Violet.

LEFT One of the alcoves that Violet designed to display china. The two-tier table that holds the drinks and glasses is by Gillow. I found it in one of the towers when we first came to the castle. The portrait is of Viscount Chaworth of Trym, by Sir Peter Lely.

RIGHT The dining table can seat up to 26 people comfortably when it is fully extended.

got the paint exactly as I wanted it, a green, that is just as good a green at night. I taught him how to rub off with a cloth the highest projections on to the last coat.' By coincidence, we painted the room a shade of pale green that appears to be similar to the colour chosen by Violet. She designed the alcoves to display china (and a few of her own Oriental pieces) and altered the once oddly shaped alcove where the sideboard is positioned. It had obviously been a huge irritation to her. *'The beautiful principal sideboard of faded mahogany tho' Empire, I could not turn out! And nothing, neither picture or mirror would fit against a wall that pitched forward from bottom even!'* Like

many a good idea, the answer emerged during dinner one evening. A friend of her son John, Sir Harry Goodhart-Rendel,[18] *'a great musician and an architect, helped me to a solution! "Make the ceiling exactly what the floor is for shape", and so it was able to take the lovely Queen Anne (or earlier) mirror bought at old George Norman's sale at Goadby when he died.'* George was a cousin of Violet's father-in-law and his mirror, a George II walnut and parcel-gilt looking glass, c.1745, still hangs where Violet left it.

Our friend, furniture specialist Orlando Rock, explained to me that the sideboard, which we always thought was made by Gillow, was actually made by another craftsman: William Wilkinson. John Martin Robinson agreed, and the archives confirmed the theory. A bill was found from the designer, J. J. Boileau, sent on 7 July 1808: 'to a design for a sideboard full size under the inspection of Mr Thoroton to be made by Wilkinson £220'. Boileau was one of the Prince Regent's designers who worked on Carlton House.

Sir Peter Lely's portraits still steal the stage in this room. I learned from Michael Hall that Lely (when he was still called Pieter van der Faes) came to London in 1641 from Holland and painted portraits of all the major and many of the minor characters at the court of Charles II. He was so successful that he employed a large number of studio assistants and his works were more often by them than the master himself. We are fortunate that all our Lely pictures are by his own hand.

Chairs from the set made for the State Dining Room were in here when we moved in, but they were heavy, especially for young children, so we sent them back where they came from. To take their place, we collected a Harlequin set of 18th-century walnut chairs from various rooms around the house and had them recovered to match the new colour scheme.

The seven-leaf Chinese screen is late 18th century and was a present to Violet from Mrs George Keppel (mistress of Edward VII) '*to improve my new room – how kind*'. It hides the entrance to the Butler's Pantry, which is now the domain of our butler, Mr Horton.

OPPOSITE Our dining room looks very much the same as it did in Violet's day. She kept the Regency furniture, but made several changes to the room. As well as adding the wall panels and display alcoves, she had the fireplace built from two old Venetian lion's heads and some very pale, fossil-free Hopton Wood limestone from the family's quarry in Derbyshire.
BELOW LEFT *The Countess of Rutland as a Shepherdess*, by Sir Peter Lely.
BELOW RIGHT *King Charles II in Garter Robes*, by the workshop of Sir Peter Lely.

THE PRIVATE DRAWING ROOM

THIS IS MY FAVOURITE family room in the castle. It is large enough to entertain fairly large numbers of guests, and small enough to be cosy. It was the first area that Violet altered and the first one I changed – just before we moved in. Eller describes it as two bachelor bedrooms with a passage in the middle leading to the terrace. It was still two rooms when Violet first saw it, but then, she writes, '*Henry took down [the] wall[s] and made it this long lovely room.*' They also raised the windows to let in more light and added panelling from Eastwell Hall, a house on the estate. The panelling was removed by my father-in-law in the 1960s (and finished up decorating the house in Derbyshire in which my brother-in-law and his wife Saskia now live). The fireplaces were copies of two at Haddon Hall; one acquired a marble surround that my father-in-law bought when the panelling went in the 1960s.

David's Aunt Ursula remembers this room when it was still panelled. The large bay window had a window seat at the bottom, and there were double doors that opened into the private Dining Room behind the display cabinet, where now there is a single door. It was furnished with the high sofas that are now in the Ballroom.

The changes that I made were small compared to those made by Violet. Ray Bradshaw, the painter with whom I have worked since I started my interior decorating business 25 years ago, distressed the walls with various layers of paint and finishes to create a subtle, faded sienna colour. The George III giltwood sofas at either end of the room came from our drawing room at Knipton Lodge (where we lived before David's father died). They were originally part of a set of six that Violet had in the Regent's Gallery. The curtains also came from our old house: we had them altered and more made to match. Like most people who inherit a large old family house, I have brought together pieces of furniture and pictures from different rooms to create my own schemes.

For a long time we thought the George II parcel-gilt display cabinets at either end of the room were from the old castle, before the 5th Duchess rebuilt it, but very little furniture survived from that time. Furniture expert Jeremy Garfield Davis thought that they probably came from Cheveley Park, the Rutlands' house near Newmarket, a belief that was confirmed later by Violet's notes. Cheveley was originally the home of the Marquis of Granby's wife, Lady Frances Seymour, and their son, the 4th Duke, inherited it. The 7th Duke sold it in 1893 and much of the furniture was brought here.

There is a striking late George II giltwood and composite figure of a Chinaman in the manner of Thomas Johnson standing in a corner of the room; I am still looking for the stand that it needs.

The Regency mahogany centre table is by Gillow and was bought by Elizabeth at the same time as a lot of other furniture in 1809. It works well in the middle of the room and always has a huge flower arrangement on it and piles of photo albums beneath it. Photographs of the children and family are also crammed on to every available space.

The pictures have all changed, and will go on changing. To the right of the fireplace is a portrait of the 4th Duke by Sir Joshua Reynolds; to the left is one of the engraver Paul du Pont (Paulus Pontius), attributed to Anthony van Dyck. Elsewhere is George Sanders' portrait of Elizabeth on a grey mare with the castle, lake and bridge in the background (see page 51).

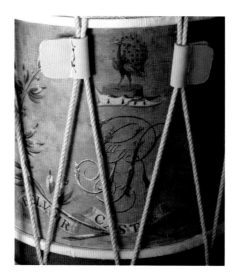

LEFT A Belvoir Castle militia drum of c.1740, adapted for use as a side table.
RIGHT The Drawing Room has excellent natural light. To the right of this photograph is a big bay window, and at the other end of the room are doors that open on to the garden terrace and views over the park beyond.
OVERLEAF The Drawing Room was once two rooms, and though I love the space, we still use it as two rooms, the desk and table acting as a divide. I find that it is vital to have various conversation areas, especially when we have lots of guests.

DAVID'S STUDY

LIKE MANY MARRIED COUPLES of their class at the time, the 5th Duke and Duchess had separate bedrooms. The Duke's bedroom was immediately below Elizabeth's and reached via a spiral staircase. The view from his window would have been almost the same as that from hers, and is the one that David enjoys today as he now uses the room as a study. The 8th Duke was the first to use it for this purpose. We didn't know what the room was used for after David's grandfather's time until we read in Violet's notebook that her husband had made his study from an old schoolroom. Maybe he had studied here as a child? The 6th and 7th Dukes had used a room adjacent to the private Drawing Room as a study but Violet knocked down the dividing wall in order to make the Drawing Room bigger, and relocated the study in what had been the 5th Duke's bedroom. Much of the furniture went at the same time, including the '*big ugly bookcase*'. She described the George III partners' desk, though, as a '*wonderfully beautiful huge table full of drawers – where always new discoveries could be made – was always the Master's Table*'. The mahogany table used for David's computer is of about the same period.

The elm desk chair is historic and is known as Wellington's Chair. A brass plate attached to the back of the seat bears the inscription: 'This chair is formed out of a tree, which in fame must be considered as surpassing every tree of the forest, being that behind the farm of La Haye Sainte, and close to which the Duke of Wellington frequently took his station during the battle of Waterloo. This tree was purchased by George Children, Esq., who kindly gave the Duke and Duchess of Rutland sufficient wood from it to form this chair; two other chairs only having been made out of it, of which, one is in the possession of his Majesty,[19] and the other was reserved by the donor for himself.' In Eller's time, it was in the Regent's Gallery but we found it in the Porter's Lodge downstairs and brought it up here.

The painting of Lady Katherine Manners, daughter of the 6th Earl of Rutland, is by Van Dyck. She married the Marquis of Buckingham, the Leicestershire-born George Villiers, in 1620 before he became the 1st Duke of Buckingham. He was the favourite courtier of James I, probably even his lover, and his rise to power had been

meteoric. Perhaps it is not surprising that her father had grave misgivings and objected to their marriage. Buckingham was killed in 1628 and Katherine married the Earl of Antrim in 1635 and went to live in Ireland.

A door links this room to what would have been the Duke's dressing room. My mother-in-law used it as her study and I use it as a small dining room for informal lunches or dinners. Over the door into the lobby is a painting by J. M. W. Turner that shows the castle as if in a fairytale, floating over the Vale, the towers and battlements awash with sunlight (see page 12).

ABOVE A Dresden mirror hangs over the fireplace in our small, informal dining room which links the private Drawing Room to David's study.
RIGHT Wellington's Chair in David's study. The room has been used as the Duke's study for four generations.

THE SPIRAL STAIRS AND LOBBIES

Many rooms sprout from corridors that widen into bulbous lobby areas at one end. These have room-like qualities – furniture, pictures and ornaments – but high windows overlooking the Courtyard and no fireplaces. They are, in most cases, oddly shaped glorified passageways but not without some identity of their own. Our private front door on the south-west terrace opens into a tiny hallway and spiral staircase that takes you up either to the lobby of our first floor-flat or on, past David's study, up to the bedroom corridor of his parents' generation that we now call Violet's Corridor.

BELOW AND RIGHT The spiral staircase that leads from the door of our private entrance to our apartments on two floors. To make the space seem more inviting, I painted it a warm, pale terracotta colour. There is a terrible temptation for children to slide down the bannister rail. The long case clock was bought in 1825.

At each floor, the stairs lead into a lobby; the first one acts as a continuation of our hallway and this is where we meet friends and offer them a drink before moving into the Drawing Room. As in the Egyptian Corridor further along, the windows overlook the dark Courtyard, so I changed the glass to mirrors to reflect internal light instead and now the lamps and chandelier give the area a warmer, welcoming atmosphere.

The second-floor lobby that leads into Violet's Corridor is outside the Libraries and some of the oldest and most valuable books in the house, collected by the 9th Duke, are displayed here in a large Regency bookcase. Nearby are Godfrey Kneller's portrait of the 1st Duchess, Catherine Noel, and a portrait of Lady Bridget Manners, daughter of 4th Earl of Rutland, by an unknown artist of the English School c.1600, which was bought by the 9th Duke in a Christie's sale.

LEFT *The Duke of Rutland's Dog Pack* (all his hounds are in the portrait), by Sir Francis Grant, outside our drawing room. The centre figure is huntsman Tom Goosey, whose hunting horn is attached to the frame.

RIGHT Our first-floor lobby is a continuation of the hallway. We replaced the glass in the arched window with 'antiqued' mirror to hide a fairly dark outlook. I used a large-print wallpaper from the Zoffany Archive collection; it looks very good with gilt frames and adds a touch of drama. The walnut bracket clock, c.1675, on the sofa table is a favourite of David's and one of many in the castle that he likes to see working.

OVERLEAF LEFT Violet's Corridor; the bathrooms that she put in lead off to the left behind the panelled doors.

OVERLEAF RIGHT The second-floor lobby leads into Violet's Corridor. The bookcase stores some of the 9th Duke's most valuable books.

VIOLET'S CORRIDOR

VIOLET CALLED THIS BEDROOM CORRIDOR the Duchess's Passage but by the time we moved in it was known as the Tangerine Corridor because it had orange walls. We changed the colour to a warm peach and named it after Violet because she added the bathrooms that lead off it. In fact we owe many of the bathrooms in the house to her. In her notebook she boasts: '*I made the bathrooms! Very proud am I to have made 12 or 14 in house and not given up one room for them!*' She managed this by building them out into the Courtyard so that they appear to be suspended above it. We have added a further six bathrooms and shower rooms to the house in the last eight years. We hung some of the pencil drawings by Violet in each of 'her' bathrooms along this corridor, partly because the ceilings are very low and can't take big pictures but mostly because it seemed to make sense. We also added curtains to the three Gothic windows to protect the furniture and books from the light.

The trio of William III chairs here with seats upholstered in needlepoint are particularly pretty; they are thought to be part of a set of six chairs bought in 1711, possibly by the 2nd Duke. The bill dated 5 May 1711 is in the archives.

BELOW One of the bathrooms that Violet added across the corridor from the bedrooms to which they now belong.
RIGHT *Robert Tyrwitt of Kettleby, Lincs*, 1601, English School, hangs outside one of Violet's bathrooms above a William III chair.
FAR RIGHT The circular bathroom, which fits snugly into one of the Chapel turrets, serves the Wyatt Bedroom. Violet decorated the walls, and the bath, in this marble-effect paper; it has weathered the storms of condensation remarkably well.

THE WYATT BEDROOM

THIS WAS ELIZABETH'S BEDROOM, or boudoir as Eller refers to it. He writes about the stunning views to be had from here, and how Elizabeth would retreat here '*whenever an intermission in the demands of her elevated rank permitted her to indulge in pursuits congenial to her highly cultivated mind*'. Blackberry Hill, seen from here, is indeed idyllic and it is where her mausoleum was built after her death in 1825. She marked her intended final resting place with two silver

fir trees; the area has become overgrown and needs cutting back so that the mausoleum can be seen more clearly.

The Regency predilection for anything Roman during this romantic period is evident in the whole room and particularly in the frieze. Eller describes the relief on the walls as '*emblematic of the elegant taste, and accomplishments, and useful pursuits, of the Duchess: – Apollo and the Muses; Minerva, and female attendants with fruit and flower; Mercury, accompanied by females holding various emblems of commerce*'. Cupid and Venus are represented in panels too.

LEFT The Roman-style frieze and cornice in the Wyatt Bedroom. RIGHT One of my father-in-law's favourite portraits, *Lord John Manners, later 7th Duke of Rutland, c.1835*, by Margaret Carpenter. BELOW One of a pair of Regency stools that were among the furniture made for this room by Morel and Hughes in 1809. OVERLEAF Much of the furniture in here was swapped with that in the Brown Bedroom by my mother-in-law. Elizabeth would barely recognize her boudoir now. But the portrait of her friend Colonel Frederick Trench above the screen may have been here and perhaps the 18th-century Venetian walnut bureau cabinet.

Soon after we moved in Mrs Plowright, the housekeeper, came to tell me that a leak had been discovered in here. Water had probably been dripping in unnoticed for weeks, and the carpet and ceiling were badly damaged. While we were making the repairs, I thought that the yellow colour of the walls didn't look right, but I wasn't brave enough at the time to change anything. Perhaps one day I will be, especially as John Martin Robinson agrees that the Wyatts would have used pale greens and greys.

Apart from a pair of rich mahogany stools by Morel and Hughes, decorated with carved and gilded dolphins by Bogaert, and a rosewood parcel-gilt fitted console table, the room is furnished quite plainly. The stools were included on the same 1809 bill as the furniture that is now in the Brown Bedroom, suggesting that originally it was all part of

the same set. The console table, however, was 'supplied to the drawing room by Morel & Hughes on May 12th 1801'. We don't know when it was brought in to the Wyatt Room although Violet refers to '*all furniture lovely English Empire – en suite*' here, so it is quite probable that it could have been here since then. She had rather a dramatic idea for the floor: '*I meant to have black & white marble floor here!! From Engine Yard.*' However, in the end she settled for a carpet – perhaps she considered how cold it would have been in winter.

A picture of Colonel Frederick Trench hangs by the fireplace. He was a close friend of the Duke of York and of Elizabeth towards the end of her life and was hugely instrumental in helping her source furniture and tapestries for the castle.

The small painting of Lord John Manners (later the 7th Duke) aged 17 by Margaret Carpenter was one of my father-in-law's favourite portraits. It is puzzling in that he is shown with his gun; when Violet, his daughter-in-law, wrote about the picture, she added, '*Lord John Manners with a gun! (he never shot!)*'.

THE BROWN BEDROOM

John Martin Robinson believes that this room, its dressing room and the Wyatt Bedroom next door are unique in as much as the furniture in this series of rooms illustrates the Prince Regent's taste so clearly and has remained so complete. Most of the furniture in this bedroom is attributed to the Royal furniture-makers Morel and Hughes; the bed, sideboard, chairs, pier glass and pot-cupboards were bought in December 1809, according to the bill in the archives. The four-poster is described on the invoice as a 'handsome State bed with cornice embellishment and various ornaments'. Having said that, my father-in-law's first wife chopped the canopy off the top of the bed when she was first married. Thankfully, his second wife, my mother-in-law, put it back again.

Most of the furniture in the dressing room was made by Gillow and the mirrored wardrobes were almost certainly made by him for this room too. Robert Gillow was a great friend of James Wyatt and they worked together on many projects; Wyatt even designed some furniture (particularly chairs) for him. Gillow used mahogany shipped from the West Indies for his furniture and Wyatt would use the off-cuts for doors and trimmings. They made a great team.

Two of the three William Marlow landscapes in the bedroom are of Italian scenes: one of Naples and another of the River Arno at Florence, and probably painted from sketches he made while on the Grand Tour in 1765–6. The third picture is of a quintessentially English scene, the River Thames, dated 1777. Michael Hall explained to me that it is painted in the Italian *vedutti* or view-painting manner associated with Canaletto and perpetuated in the English

RIGHT ABOVE We have recently replaced the bed hangings, including the starburst inside the canopy.
RIGHT BELOW *A View of Florence with Bridge over the Arno*, by William Marlow. It was bought by the 4th Duke for £40.
OPPOSITE The suite of Regency mahogany and parcel gilt furniture by Morel and Hughes was originally supplied for Elizabeth's boudoir, which is now the Wyatt Bedroom. If the bed wasn't so enormous and difficult to handle I would be tempted to move it back again, along with the rest of the furniture that was bought for the Wyatt Bedroom.

School of painting by Samuel Scott, Marlow's first teacher. It shows the Thames from the south bank at Southwark, looking north across to St Paul's Cathedral during the Great Frost of 1776. As Marlow was a great friend of Sir Joshua Reynolds this picture was probably bought directly from the artist by Lord Granby on Reynolds' advice, after it was displayed at the Society of Artists' annual exhibition at Spring Gardens, Charing Cross, during the year it was painted. The two Italian views were bought for £30, but the price of the London scene is unrecorded.

The late David Hicks decorated the room in the 1960s. Since then, very little has been changed: a border with a Roman key design has been added to the curtain, and the chairs have been recovered in new material. Hicks's brown and yellow scheme is very striking, but one day we may change the rather dark, heavy brown for a lighter colour that would better reflect the Regency period.

THE TAPESTRY ROOM

AT THE END of Violet's Corridor is the Tapestry Room. It is part of the private side of the house, but on the occasions that it is used for special displays or exhibitions, it is open to the public. Conveniently, it can also be reached from the Ballroom. It has probably been redecorated more times than any other room, demonstrating how fashions have changed over the last two hundred years. Other than adding a shower in a cupboard, for the convenience of guests who sleep here, I have done very little. In 2007 it was the subject of a complete makeover for the Jean-Marc Vallée film *Young Victoria*. The props department made the bed that was used by Emily Blunt, who plays the Queen. The rest of the furniture, including a very pretty Charles II giltwood side table, and the Regency rosewood day bed made by Gillow, were left on set, but the three Mortlake tapestries, after which the room is named, were temporarily removed during filming. Ironically, before Queen Victoria visited the castle in 1843, the 5th Duke considered the room for the Royal party but decided it was unsuitable.

Eller called it the Green Room or Assembling Room and describes it as '*an apartment in which the family and visitors at the Castle assemble, previous to dinner*'. In his time it was furnished with green satin damask, and green wallpaper on which hung the seven *Sacraments* by Nicolas Poussin. There are now only five: one of the paintings was burnt in the 1816 fire, and David's grandfather sold another to pay death duties. The remaining pictures were moved round the castle and hung in various rooms before being sent to the National Gallery, but on loan, in 2001.

Violet called this room the Corner Room. In her father-in-law's day it was known as the White Room, having been named for the colour of the silk from Rome with which her husband's aunt, Lady Adeliza Norman, had covered the walls and made the curtains, presumably for her father, the 5th Duke, during his widowerhood. Violet hung the three late-17th-century Mortlake tapestries of *The Naked Boys* here in 1925. Textile historian Annabel

OPPOSITE The Tapestry Room was used as the new Queen's bedroom in the film *Young Victoria*, and the four-poster bed was made for the set. We were able to buy the bed when filming was finished; it makes rather a good feature in the room and is probably far more comfortable than the one in which our guests had to sleep before.
BELOW LEFT 'VR' is embroidered on the headboard.
BELOW CENTRE *Bridget, Wife of 3rd Duke of Rutland*, 1717, by Michael Dahl.
BELOW RIGHT A close-up of the new bed gives its age away.

Westman informed me that in the 17th century Belvoir Castle was rich in tapestry hangings. An inventory taken in 1645 recorded 18 pieces in the Great Chamber alone, with a total of 45 pieces being noted in 1654. Many were later stored at Haddon Hall, of which around 60 were destroyed in a fire in 1925. Some, including *The Naked Boys*, were rescued and brought to Belvoir. The 8th Countess of Rutland, who was related to Sir Gilbert Pickering, director of Mortlake during the middle years of the 17th century, purchased these and other sets in the collection.

Violet notes that Janetta, the 7th Duke's second wife, brought the two lovely mirrors and console tables here from the Regent's Gallery. The carpet came from Cheveley and did duty in the Guard Room before settling here.

BELOW *The Naked Boys*, in the series of the 17th-century Mortlake tapestries that Violet hung in this room in 1925.
RIGHT On the left is a Charles II gilded side table with a beautiful scrolled frame carved with putti and ancanthus foliage; it would have been a stand for a cabinet. Two rather disappointing wardrobes obscure the view of the tapestry and need moving.

THE WELLINGTON ROOM

THIS ROOM belongs to the Chinese Rooms, but is not open to the public. It is named after the bed that the Duke of Wellington used on his many visits to Belvoir. The bed was in a suite of rooms on the floor below, but was moved up here by Janetta, the second wife of the 7th Duke. In Violet's day the room was known as the Ambassadors' Room, since all the ambassadors who stayed at the castle during her time at Belvoir slept here. But Eller called it a '*Sitting room*', an annex to the Chinese Bedroom and Dressing Room, which was its original purpose. '*Though of unusual shape,*' he said he found it '*a very agreeable apartment*', and goes on to say, '*the character of the room is preserved in the paper, in the covers of the chairs, couches, etc. which are adorned with flowers worked in coloured silks, on a bright yellow ground.*'

One of the curiosities in this room is the cheese in the glass dome. In 1825 the Duke of York made a speech in the House of Lords on behalf of the Protestant ascendancy in Ireland. He defended the Protestant cause with such eloquence that the Protestant cheesemakers of Cheshire presented him with an enormous cheese, '149 weight (the largest ever made)' the label states, by way of thanks. The Duke of York presented a piece to Mary Isabella, the Dowager Duchess, and it was preserved by Professor Cumming. I slept here the night before I married David, and looking at it, I thought it made an interesting bedfellow for a bride before her wedding day.

RIGHT Although the bed was used by the Duke of Wellington when he stayed at the castle, it was moved in here only a decade or so after his death. The bed itself, of swagged and pierced mahogany, is attributed to Marsh and Tatham, cabinet-makers who made the furniture for the Prince Regent's pavilion in Brighton. The pink silk upholstery was done during my mother-in-law's day. The Chinese wallpaper is probably the only remaining element of the original decorative scheme. The Regency rosewood ebony parcel-gilt and lacquer wardrobe, c.1810, attributed to Morel and Hughes was brought here by Violet and is one of a pair. The other one is in the King's Bedroom.

LEFT David found this picture of The Duke of Wellington in a storeroom and hung it above 'The Cheese'.

The Regency rosewood and ebony parcel-gilt and lacquer wardrobe is attributed to Morel and Hughes and dates from about 1810; it was brought here by Violet from another bedroom. She bought the gilt brackets on the wall near the bed and fireplace but doesn't say where from. In her notebook she writes about a screen in the Ambassadors' Room: '*(very common) but I used to have on it a wonderful green counterpane – I used it for my little boy's recumbent statue and that is why I must not leave it behind me – if ever I leave alive.*' She thought a lot of things were common but to write about its reason for being there is rather poignant.

The Chippendale chest came from Cheveley; Violet put it under the window. She bought the scarlet and gilt lacquered screen by the door from Italy, but her best contribution is the bathroom, which makes for a much quicker dash in the middle of the night. We repapered it recently; it wasn't easy finding a wallpaper to resemble the old Chinese paper but very satisfying to buy this one from an American company.

OPPOSITE ABOVE The door on the right opens into the bathroom.
OPPOSITE BELOW LEFT Decorative Chinese items team with the wallpaper.
OPPOSITE BELOW RIGHT A collection of material relating to Wellington includes a letter addressed to the Duchess of Rutland, dated April 1825, from Wellington's address in the Albany, and a bracelet with a cameo of his profile.
ABOVE LEFT A detail of the wallpaper.
ABOVE RIGHT Violet created the bathroom in the early 1900s, and we have recently redecorated it. The drawing is one of Violet's, but the sitter is unknown.

Epilogue

Living in Today's Castle

No previous generation of the Manners family would fully recognize life in the castle today. The halcyon days of vast numbers of staff, spectacular entertaining and the aristocracy's assumed place in society have long gone. The effects of death duties, introduced at the end of the 19th century, fewer people going into service after the Second World War and a fluctuating economy are just some of the many contributory factors that make it necessary for Belvoir, like many other houses of its kind, to run as a viable business and not just as a private family home.

In reality we are not so different from our forbears who fought to save the castle and its heritage for future generations. The battles of today may not be bloody but the house has enemies such as dry rot, damp and general external and internal decay. We have to nurture our relationships with the tax man, the bank manager and the health and safety officer just as earlier generations nurtured theirs with the church authorities or the Court.

When David inherited the dukedom, my first priority was to create an intimate family home for ourselves and our four children (Hugo, our youngest, had yet to make an appearance). I had had an idyllic childhood on my parents' farm in Wales; dogs, ponies, friends, family and laughter

were our staple diet, and I was keen to recreate a similar environment for my own children. Family life has always been very important to me. It took six months to convert the old Nursery wing to our central-heated, self-contained flat. For the first time in the castle's history the family shares a relatively small living space that centres on a kitchen. An Aga would complete the picture but the floor would have had to have been reinforced and the budget would have been blown to pieces.

In August 2001 we moved into the castle from Knipton Lodge, a charming six-bedroom Georgian house on the edge of the park. For me, the challenges were formidable. As the last removal man left, and my mother-in-law was about to depart too, she handed me a large box of keys, looked me in the eye and said, 'Good luck'. For David, it was merely coming home and he didn't give the move a second's thought. But for the children, particularly the older ones, moving to Granny and Grandpa's huge old pile was not so much an adventure as a terrifying prospect. Getting lost, a fear of ghosts, the freezing cold of the main part of the house in winter and sharing their toys and moods with the public and office staff were just some of the hurdles to be overcome. These days, they still comment that it takes seven minutes to answer the door bell and that income-generating discos for other people's parties keep them awake at night, but pop stars staying the night after concerts in the park, the occasional Hollywood film crew on location and enough space to entertain all their friends in one go more than make up for it. They all appreciate, and are very proud of, the special place in which they live.

The Speak-a-Word Room leads off the Pre-Guard Room. Originally it was the place where the 5th Duke came for brief meetings with tenants or staff – hence its name. Since then it has been staff rooms and visitors' cloakrooms and then became my office in 2006. The skylight throws valuable natural light on to our working day.

Our first job was to ascertain exactly what we had taken on. A full survey of the castle was carried out, from the chimney pots to the drains. The report that came back specified that a startling £6.5 million needed to be spent almost immediately in order to prevent further decay in the hot spots that had been highlighted. The roof was rotting, the drains were disintegrating and the lead in the windows was breaking up. As an interior decorator, I had spent most of my working life finding the right people to help me, but drains were not my speciality (and James Wyatt's drains are deeply complicated), and properties of lead were not foremost in my mind either. As I found to our cost, however, if you get such basic things wrong, you get into far greater trouble. When we re-roofed the Speak-a-Word Room that is now my office, I chose the wrong roofers; the result was that all the lead had to be stripped off and different builders had to start again.

We learned from our mistake, and employed a sympathetic architect from Grantham who had a lot of experience renovating churches, cathedrals and other historic houses. With his help, re-roofing the State Dining Room was, by comparison, much easier and also considerably cheaper than the report had estimated. After the roof was done we tackled the lead in the windows, and now there isn't much I don't know about lead. I wonder if any previous Duchess of Rutland could have said the same?

The learning curve was steep to begin with, and we have never stopped learning. We had been here for about three weeks when the children burst into our bedroom very early one morning and announced that water was pouring down the walls in our lobby area outside our Drawing Room and into the Libraries below. Realizing that heavy rainfall overnight must be causing the damage, I pulled on my Barbour over my nightie, yanked on my wellies and made my way up to the roof, several children in tow. Fortunately it didn't take too long to discover that a dead pigeon had blocked a drain. Unfortunately I had to slide down the lead roof on my bottom and dig it out with my bare hands to clear it. The whole experience was highly amusing for my giggling brood, but rewarding for me in that that dead pigeon taught me a lot.

Pigeon excrement rots lead and causes leaks. The best way to deal with pigeons is to deter them from roosting on the roof in the first place. We have since resorted to the old tried-and-tested method of installing birds of prey in close proximity to them. In our case that is the Courtyard. Our resident pigeon population is now on the decline and, as an added bonus, we have included birds of prey demonstrations among our visitor attractions in the summer.

That one pigeon caused considerable water damage to some of the books in the Libraries. In order to deal with this, we contacted the local branch of NADFAS. That invaluable organization provided volunteers to clean – and then catalogue – the books, and that experience, thankfully, developed into a 16-year restoration programme that benefits both parties.

Every autumn when the house closes its doors to the public, the builders and restorers return. £100,000 will be spent annually on restoration for the next 20 years. Skilled stonemasons are scheduled to start work on the pinnacles above the Chapel, and by 2011 major repairs to the retaining walls will have been started and re-wiring and replacing the lead pipes in the plumbing system will have begun. Many of the windows need repairing and restoring: a job that will require an in-house joiner and will have to be done in phases over several years.

Annual spring cleaning starts as soon as the last of the Christmas trees are removed and takes the best part of three months to complete. Work begins on the top floors of the towers where generations of 'stuff', rather loosely described as 'storage', has been dumped. Every room is swept, windows are cleaned and any furniture is polished and re-covered with dust sheets. The public rooms also get head-to-toe treatment. Scaffolding is erected to clean the high ceilings except those that are particularly ornate and gilded, which are therefore cleaned once every five years. Every window is washed, the fires are swept and black-leaded, the furniture is polished and the floors are cleaned and sealed, and the soft furnishings are beaten or vacuumed. On top of this, the guns and swords in the Guard Room, the crystal chandeliers, and the silver and

FAR LEFT Peacocks on the roof outside the 40-Acre Landing.
LEFT The castle roof covers nearly 2½ acres. The Gothic shaped Ballroom windows are to the left of the Courtyard and the roof of the Libraries, to the right of the picture, is where a build-up of pigeon excrement caused a costly leak.
RIGHT ABOVE Volunteers from NADFAS cataloguing and restoring books in the main library.
RIGHT BELOW The castle's duty manager, Sallyann Jackson, cleaning one of the Waterford crystal chandeliers in the Regent's Gallery as part of the annual spring clean.

china require specialized cleaning. Household cleaning also involves conservation, particularly on fragile textiles. Our textile specialist carries out a lot of the general work but important pieces like the early 19th-century carpet in the Elizabeth Saloon and the Mortlake tapestries require extremely careful and specialist attention. The cycle of claeaning and repairing is never-ending.

When my father-in-law died in 1999, David's inheritance tax bill was £9 million, and the legal bills involved in settling this over the next seven years amounted to about £100,000 a year. In order to keep the bulk of the collections together we decided to offer an important painting by Van Dyck, *Charles I and the Procession of the Order of the Garter*, and a set of valuable miniatures to the nation in lieu of death duties. (The Van Dyck is now on permanent view at the Ashmolean Museum in Oxford.) Now the castle's basic running costs, including utility bills, staffing and general maintenance, add up to about half a million pounds each year. The wherewithal to fund this comes largely from castle and park events. Ticket money from visitors during the season when the house is open is not enough these days. My father-in-law regularly welcomed 100,000 tourists per season; by comparison, in 2008 we saw only 25,000. Many historic houses have seen a steady decline in numbers over the last few years. I believe that Sunday shopping, multi-channels on television, theme parks and cheap flights to holiday destinations probably have something to do with this. But we are very lucky that other income-generating opportunities have arisen to compensate for decreasing visitor numbers, and we have seen a healthy increase in corporate hospitality, weddings and pop concerts. The wear and tear on a house is far greater than on parkland, which by and large repairs itself, so outside attractions are more popular from our point of view. But we continue to strike a balance and try to accommodate all opportunities.

It would be only too easy to go on about how much everything costs but living at Belvoir isn't all about balance sheets. We love living here; it is a great privilege to wake up every morning and look out over immaculate gardens to unspoilt views; to be surrounded by many breathtaking works of art in a home that never runs out of

OPPOSITE ABOVE The new Shoot Room doubles as a corporate dining room or meeting room.

OPPOSITE BELOW The Guard Room, set up for a wedding.

TOP LEFT *Hound Exercise*, by Sir Alfred Munnings.

TOP RIGHT The kennels for the Belvoir hounds were built in the early 19th century to James Wyatt's designs. The octagonal roof absorbs the noise made by hounds. Not much has changed. Here Belvoir huntsman George Grant is leading the hounds out for their daily exercise.

BOTTOM LEFT The Charles II stable block was built in 1660 at the same time as the third castle. The indoor riding ring was added in the late 19th century and is one of only four like it in the country.

BOTTOM RIGHT An Arab horse, owned by my mother-in-law, stands at one of the gates to the Kitchen Garden designed by James Wyatt in the early years of the 19th century.

ABOVE LEFT David and I look through an old ledger in the Muniment Room with John Granger, our archivist.

ABOVE RIGHT Mr Horton has been the family butler for 18 years.

OPPOSITE Our family portrait, set in the Ballroom, and painted in 2008 by the Russian artist Vasili Smirnov. Standing, from the left: Eliza, Alice, David, self; sitting: our dog Daisy, lying down, Violet, Charles, Hugo, and our chocolate Labrador Nelson.

space and also to feel a part of over nine hundred years of one family's history. We face different challenges every day but essentially life at the castle is hugely enjoyable. It was built for fun and living here is still fun.

I find myself constantly wondering how Elizabeth, wife of the 5th Duke, would have coped in the castle today. Would she have rolled her sleeves up and dealt with changing circumstances in order to secure her home for future generations, or would she have thrown up her hands, sold up and taken the money? I have no doubt that she would have taken the former route, driven – as she was – by a strong love for her family as well as by ruthless determination. There could have been no greater blow to her than the disastrous fire in 1816 that threatened not just her building ambitions, but also the lives of her children (see page 49). Despite everything – not least the unimaginable frustrations, the irreplaceable losses and an ever-increasing financial burden, she gritted her teeth and continued with her plans to build one of the finest houses in the country for her husband's family. I have learned a great deal from her: to trust my instincts, cherish an unconditional love for my family and try never to lose sight of the positive in everything.

We are eternally grateful to our dedicated team of staff that steers us forward to achieve what has been the prime objective of every generation of Rutlands: to pass on the castle and estate in sound health to the next heir. No one knows what the rest of the 21st century holds for us, or how it will affect historic houses and their families. I believe firmly that those who are most passionate about their family homes will continue to make the best curators, and I am confident that Belvoir will see its millennium anniversary in 2067.

Notes

All quotes in the text that are not credited with sources below come from the Belvoir Archives.

PARALLEL LIVES (PAGES 14–75)

1 Diana Cooper, *The Rainbow Comes and Goes,* Rupert Hart-Davis, 1958. Lady Diana Manners married Duff Cooper, 1st Viscount Norwich, politician, cabinet minister, diplomat, writer and diarist.

2 Ian Kelly, *Beau Brummell – The Ultimate Dandy,* Hodder & Stoughton, 2005.

3 Francis Bamford and the Duke of Wellington, ed., *The Journal of Mrs. Arbuthnot, 1820–1832,* Macmillan, 1950. Mrs Arbuthnot, wife of Charles Arbuthnot MP (who was 26 years her senior), was a diarist, social observer and political hostess on behalf of the Tory party. She was a regular visitor to Belvoir, accompanying her husband's great friend the Duke of Wellington and described as his 'closest woman friend'.

4 During their early life together the 5th Duke and Duchess had lodgings on Lower Grosvenor Street.

5 Wilsford Hall, near Ancaster.

6 Rosemary Baird, *Mistress of the House: Great Ladies and Grand Houses 1670–1830,* Weidenfeld & Nicolson, 2003.

7 Francis Bamford and the Duke of Wellington, *op. cit.*

8 Manuscripts of the Duke of Rutland, volume I, p. xiii.

9 Lawrence Stone, *Family and Fortune: Studies in Aristocratic Finance in the Sixteenth and Seventeenth Centuries,* Oxford University Press, 1973.

10 Michael Honeybone, *Wicked Practise and Sorcerye,* 2008.

11 She was a staunch Protestant who would have influenced her husband.

12 The Revd Irvin Eller, *The History of Belvoir Castle,* 1841.

13 The Revd Irvin Eller, *op. cit.*

14 George's fourth son, Charles Manners-Sutton (1755–1828), grandson of the 3rd Duke, served as Archbishop of Canterbury from 1805 to 1828. His son, Charles Manners-Sutton (1814–35), was created 1st Viscount Canterbury and allowed his name to be put forward for Prime Minister in 1832 in an anti-reform ministry. He was voted out of the Speaker's chair by the Whigs.

15 Walter Evelyn Manners, *Some Account of the Military, Political and Social Life of the Right Hon John Manners, Marquis of Granby,* Macmillan and Co. Ltd, 1899.

16 T. F. Dale, *The History of the Belvoir Hunt,* Archibald Constable and Company, 1899.

17 J. Nichols, *The History and Antiquities of the County of Leicestershire,* 1795.

18 Sir Nathaniel William Wraxall, *The Historical and Posthumous Memoirs of Sir Nathaniel William Wraxall 1772–1784,* H. B. Wheatley, 1884.

19 Crabbe was a naturalist and a poet whose literary friends included William Wordsworth and Sir Walter Scott.

20 Mary Lyons, ed., *The Memoirs of Mrs Leeson, Madam 1727–1797,* Lilliput Press, 1995.

21 George John Frederick Manners, Marquis of Granby, born 20 August 1813 in Lower Grosvenor Street, London, died 15 June 1814 at Belvoir.

22 In a letter to the Marchioness of Salisbury, Elizabeth explained that news of scarlet fever was prevalent in Newmarket at the time and she had therefore decided to leave the children at Belvoir.

23 Rosemary Baird, *op. cit.*

24 She replaced Georgiana, Duchess of Devonshire, in the scandalous dandy Beau Brummell's affections early on in her marriage. He was a bad influence on her husband's younger brothers, Lords Charles and Robert, the 'bad Manners' who followed him into debt gambling. The Duke of Rutland did not like him and his friendship with Elizabeth fizzled out.

25 Francis Bamford and the Duke of Wellington, *op. cit.*

26 The Revd Irvin Eller, *op. cit.*

27 James Yorke, 'Belvoir Castle, Leicestershire 11', *Country Life,* 39 June 30 1994.

28 Designed and built by Benjamin Wyatt.

29 T. F. Dale, *op.cit.*

30 Guy Paget and Lionel Irvine, *Leicestershire, The County Books Series,* Robert Hale, 1950.

31 Edward Pearce, ed., *The Diaries of Charles Greville,* Pimlico Books, 2005.

32 Lord George Bentinck and Disraeli led the protectionists within the Conservative party to try to prevent the repeal of the Corn Laws.

33 Edward Pearce, *op. cit.*

34 Nearly 30 years later, in 1873, and aged 54, Selina (who was still married to Lord Bradford) became the focus of widower Benjamin Disraeli's affections. Having known her and her sister Anne, Lady Chesterfield, through Granby and his brother Lord John, since their youth, Disraeli found himself suddenly in love with them both, even proposing to the widowed Anne, who turned him down. He remained close to Selina until his death in 1881.

35 The Countess of Cardigan and Lancastre, *My Recollections*, Everleigh House, 1909.

36 Diana Cooper, *op. cit.*

37 Leslie Stephen and Sidney Lee, *Dictionary of National Biography*, 63 vols., 1885–1900.

38 William Flavelle Monypenny and George Earle Buckle, *The Life of Benjamin Disraeli, Earl of Beaconsfield*, Russell & Russell, 1968.

39 Charles Whibley, *Lord John Manners and his Friends*, William Blackwood and Sons, 1905.

40 Diana Cooper, *op. cit.*

41 Diana Cooper, *op. cit.*

42 *The Times*, 11 October 2008.

MY TOUR (PAGES 76–209)

1 The Revd Irvin Eller, *The History of Belvoir Castle*, 1841. I am indebted to Michael Honeybone for the following notes he has supplied on the life of the Revd Eller. Joseph Irvin Eller (1800–77) was born in Great Yarmouth, Norfolk, the oldest of the eight children of Joseph Eller and Margaret, née Irvin. His education is unconfirmed, but in the frontispiece of *The History of Belvoir Castle* he states that he was 'of Queen's College, Cambridge [University]'. During the 1830s and 1840s he lived in the Grantham area, close to Belvoir Castle, and was probably curate or priest responsible first for Heydour Church and then for St Sebastian's Church, Great Gonerby. During the early 1840s Eller was actively involved in the establishment of the Lincolnshire Architectural and Archæological Society, which is now the Society for Lincolnshire History and Archæology. From 1848 until his death, Eller was Rector of Faldingworth.

2 Diana Cooper, *op. cit.*

3 We are grateful to military expert Stephen Wood for the following information about the guidons and the Light Dragoons. The Light Dragoons first made their appearance in the British Army in 1756, as single troops of light horse attached to existing cavalry regiments. Their role was chiefly to act as skirmishers and reconnaissance troops, and they were so successful that seven regiments of Light Dragoons were raised in 1759 and 1760, John Granby raising the 21st with effect from 5 April 1760 and being appointed its colonel. The soldiers were armed with light dragoon pattern pistols – 21st Light Dragoons having their own particular pattern – and long light swords with straight singled-edged blades and rudimentary hilts; their distinctive headdress was a 'Roman' helmet with a flowing horsehair plume and a metal frontal plate. The 21st Light Dragoons never served abroad and were disbanded in Nottingham in 1763. Several other cavalry regiments with the number 21st were subsequently raised but none had any connection with Lord Granby's 21st Light Dragoons of 1760–63.

Guidons are a type of short, swallow-tailed standard. On parade and in battle, the guidons would have been carried by the most junior officers – those of the rank of cornet – each of whom would have been protected by two non-commissioned officers to prevent the guidons being captured. At Belvoir the three preserved guidons of the 21st Dragoons are the scarlet First, or King's guidon, with a crowned Union Spray (the conjoined Rose of England and the Thistle of Scotland) in its centre and the Second and Third guidons with the King's cypher GR (for Georgius Rex, or King George) in the centre. Each guidon would have been allocated to a squadron of the regiment

4 Francis Bamford and the Duke of Wellington, *op. cit.*

5 James Yorke, 'Belvoir Castle, Leicester', *Country Life*, 30 June 1994. The bills for this consignment are now missing from the archive but James Yorke allowed Annabel access to the research notes that he had taken from the archive in preparation for his article to help with this book.

6 James Yorke, *op. cit.*

7 Christopher Hussey, 'Belvoir Castle, Leicestershire', *Country Life*, 20 December 1956.

8 James Yorke, *op. cit.* The carpet bills are also missing.

9 Sarah B. Sherill, *Carpets and Rugs of Europe and America*, Abbeville Press, 1996.

10 James Yorke, *op. cit.*

11 James Yorke, *op. cit.*

12 James Yorke, *op. cit.*

13 Geoffrey Beard and Annabel Westman, 'A French Upholsterer Working in England: Francis Lapiere, 1653–1714', *The Burlington Magazine*, vol. CXXXV, no. 1085 (August 1993), pp. 515–24.

14 Geoffrey Beard and Annabel Westman, *op. cit.*

15 P. Glanville, *Silver in Tudor and Early Stuart England*, 1900.

16 Charissa Bremer-David, *French Tapestries & Textiles in the J. Paul Getty Museum*, J. Paul Getty Museum, 1997.

17 Charissa Bremer-David, *op. cit.*

18 Chairman of the Architectural Association, owner of Hatchlands, Surrey (National Trust).

19 In the Guard Room at Windsor Castle.

Index

Page numbers in *italics* refer to captions to illustrations

Picture Credits

The authors and publishers would like to thank the
photographers whose work appears on the following pages:

Nick McCann 1–4, 10, 14, 17–20, 21 right, 22–38, 40–46,
48–51, 52 left, 53, 54 top, 55–69, 70 top, 71 right, 72, 74 bottom,
75, 80–1, 95, 97 bottom, 98, 100, 101 right, 106, 110 top left and
bottom left, 111, 114–115, 118–120, 122 left, 123, 125 top, 127
right, 128, 130, 131, 144–145, 148 left and centre, 149, 150–153,
154 left and right, 155 left, 158–164, 166–177, 179–181, 184,
186–191, 193–195, 198–200, 202–203, 205–206, 208 bottom
right, 209 right, 212 left, 214, 215 top left, 216 right.

Jane Pruden 21 left.

Rupert Watts 5, 9, 47, 52 right, 70 bottom, 76–79, 82–85,
88–90, 92–94, 96, 97 top left, centre and right, 99, 101 left,
102–105, 107–109, 110 top right and bottom right, 112,
116–7, 121, 122 right, 125 bottom, 126 bottom, 132–143, 145,
147, 148 right, 152, 154 centre, 155 right, 156–7, 165, 178,
183, 185, 192, 196–7, 201, 204, 207, 208 top and left, 209 left,
210, 212 right, 213, 215 top right, bottom left and right, 216
left, 217, endpapers.

All other photographs come from the Belvoir archives.

Ground plans on pages 86–7 by Becky Clarke.

Author's Acknowledgments

I AM ENORMOUSLY GRATEFUL to everyone who helped me to further my journey of discovery around the castle. Learning more about the architecture, the collections and all the people who have lived here before us has been both compelling and a privilege. My first thank yous go to my husband David, and to my children, Violet, Alice, Eliza, Charles and Hugo, for suffering my occasional distance as I absorbed yet another milestone in the castle's creation. A big thank you, too, to my sister-in-law, Charlotte, for her kind loan of photographs and to my mother-in-law, Frances, the Dowager Duchess of Rutland, whose knowledge of the castle has been a greatly appreciated source of reference.

Compiling the book has been a steep learning curve and one that I could not have considered without huge support and time from many experts. John Martin Robinson, historian and author, continues to fire my enthusiasm for all things to do with the Wyatts. Orlando Rock and Jeremy Garfield Davies (who also helped to gather some of the specialists together for me) have helped identify many of the pieces of furniture in both our private apartment and the public areas. Annabel Westman's unstoppable and infectious knowledge of textiles has given me a whole new perspective on tapestries, carpets and beds. John Morton Morris, Michael Hall and Sir John Guinness completely re-educated me about the pictures; Lucy Morton lent her support to our silver collection; Elle Shusan lent hers to the miniatures; military specialist Stephen Wood explained, in great detail, the importance of the firearms, and Tim Knox, former head curator of the National Trust, has given me a terrific overview of the castle.

Dr Michael Honeybone is an historian who knows more about the people who have lived in the castle than anyone I know and we are hugely indebted to his invaluable help and the time he spent checking the manuscript for historical accuracy as we went a long. We were very lucky to meet Fiona Torrens-Spence who kindly helped with research into the lives of the 5th, 6th and 7th Earls of Rutland while she researched her own book about the 6th Earl's daughter, Katherine Manners, later Duchess of Buckingham.

Several of our Guides deserve a special thank you. John Daybell has been tireless in his efforts to research many of the lives of the earlier occupants; Brian Howes also contributed to some of the earlier history; and Margaret Ashley's reading and checking has been a great comfort.

Without our Archivist, John Granger, to delve into the endless filing cabinets in the Muniment Rooms for evidence, letters, dates and anything of interest over the last 942 years, the book would never have got off the ground. His discovery of the notebook made by Violet, the 8th Duchess of Rutland, completely altered the course of the book.

Robert Hildyard kindly allowed us to photograph some of his family portraits and supplied us with evidence about relationships between both families. The childhood memories of David's uncle and aunt, Lord Roger Manners and Lady Ursula D'Abo, enriched the chapters about the 8th and 9th Dukes: thank you.

Rupert Watts and Nick McCann have brought all the stories to life with their photographs. Other thanks must go to the Duty Manager Sallyann Jackson, my P.A., Victoria Walton, the Castle Manager, Simon Foster, and to Phil O'Brien and Harvey Proctor. I am grateful to Jonathan Harington, who kindly looked up his own family's history to help with a story about the civil war, to Steffie Shields who is a much-valued Lancelot 'Capability' Brown expert; to gardener and historian Timothy Clark for his knowledge of the gardens, and to Julie Wilson-Dyer-Gough whose idea to do a book inspired the project in the first place.

Publisher John Nicoll's encouragement and patience, the expertise of the editorial team at Frances Lincoln, and designer Anne Wilson's extraordinary skill in reproducing the essence of the castle from thousands of photographs have all contributed to what has been a thoroughly enjoyable experience.

By far my greatest debt of thanks, however, goes to Jane Pruden, friend and freelance writer, and her family. I eventually persuaded her to write the book with me, and it would never have seen the light of day but for her heroic efforts.

Emma Rutland, Belvoir Castle, 2009